W9-BZU-832

PLANNING FOR QUALITY, PRODUCTIVITY, AND COMPETITIVE POSITION

PLANNING FOR QUALITY, PRODUCTIVITY, AND COMPETITIVE POSITION

Howard S. Gitlow
Executive Director
University of Miami Institute for the Study of Quality in Manufacturing and Service
University of Miami
Coral Gables, Florida

and

Process Management International, Inc.
Bloomington, Minnesota

Dow Jones-Irwin
Homewood, Illinois 60430

Sponsoring editor: Jeffrey A. Krames
Project editor: Karen J. Murphy
Production manager: Ann Cassady
Compositor: Arcata Graphics/Kingsport
Typeface: 11/13 Century Schoolbook
Printer: R. R. Donnelley & Sons Company

Library of Congress Cataloging-in-Publication Data

Gitlow, Howard S.
Planning for quality, productivity, and competitive position / by Howard S. Gitlow and Process Management International, Inc.
p. cm.
Includes bibliographical references.
ISBN 1-55623-357-4
ISBN 1-55623-466-X (ASQC Edition)
1. Quality assurance. 2. Quality control—Statistical methods.
I. Process Management International, Inc. II. Title.
TS156.6.G57 1990
658.5′62—dc20 90–31206
CIP

Printed in the United States of America
1 2 3 4 5 6 7 8 9 0 DO 7 6 5 4 3 2 1 0

PREFACE

Are you frustrated with your organization's attempts toward the improvement of quality? Do you know what to do next in your quality improvement efforts, or are you floundering, with no clear plan? This book will provide insight into improving quality in your organization.

This book presents seven tools which help managers and engineers to develop quality improvement plans by specifying all required actions, necessary personnel, work load balancing, time sequencing, and contingency plans for potential problems. These tools form an integrated system for resolving difficult problems which have not responded to traditional methods, such as, "What must management do to get rid of organizational barriers to quality improvement?" Additional applications of the seven management tools are policy management, quality function deployment, new product or process development (including innovation), product or process modification, and project planning.

Appreciation goes to Michael Brassard of GOAL/QPC, Margaret Reydel, and the Quality Improvement Department of Florida Power and Light Company for their contributions to the authors' knowledge of the seven management tools. Special thanks go to Lori L. Silverman and Annabeth Probst, both of Process Management International (PMI), for their contributions to the content of this book, and to the PMI Product Development staff for their diligent work on this book.

Howard S. Gitlow
and
Process Management International, Inc.

CONTENTS

LIST OF FIGURES

PLANNING FOR QUALITY, PRODUCTIVITY, AND COMPETITIVE POSITION

CHAPTER 1

FUNDAMENTALS OF QUALITY, PRODUCTIVITY, AND COMPETITIVE POSITION

THE HISTORY OF QUALITY[1,2,3]

Issues of quality have existed since tribal chiefs, kings, and pharaohs ruled. The Code of Hammurabi, dating from 2150 B.C., states, "If a builder has built a house for a man, and his work is not strong, and the house falls in and kills the householder, that builder shall be slain." Phoenician inspectors eliminated any repeated violations of quality standards by chopping off the hand of the maker of the defective product. Inspectors accepted or rejected products and enforced government specifications. In about 1450 B.C., Egyptian inspectors checked the squareness of stone blocks with a string as the stonecutter watched. The Aztecs in Central America also used this method. These ancient civilizations emphasized equity of trade and complaint handling.

During the 13th century A.D., apprenticeships and guilds developed. The craftsmen were both trainers and inspectors. They knew their trades, their products, and their customers, and they built quality into their goods. They took pride in their work and in training others to do quality work. The government set and provided standards (for example, weights and measures), and, in most cases an individual could inspect all the products and establish a single quality standard. This idyllic state of quality could thrive in a small, localized world, but the world's growing population demanded more products.

With the birth of the Industrial Revolution, mass production of manufactured goods became possible through the division of labor and the creation of interchangeable parts. However, this created problems for those accustomed to having their goods tailor-made.

The modern industrial system began to emerge at the end of the 19th century. In the United States, Frederick Taylor pioneered scientific management, removing work planning from the job responsibilities of workers and foremen and placing it in the hands of industrial engineers. The 20th century ushered in a technical era that enabled the masses to obtain products previously reserved for the wealthy. Henry Ford introduced the moving assembly line into the manufacturing environment of Ford Motor Company. Assembly line production divided complex operations into simple procedures that could be performed by unskilled labor, resulting in highly technical products at low cost. Part of this process was an inspection to separate nonconforming and conforming products. Quality was viewed as the sole responsibility of the manufacturing department.

Soon it became apparent that the production manager's priority was meeting manufacturing deadlines rather than being concerned with quality. He would lose his job if he didn't meet production demands, whereas he would only be reprimanded if quality was poor. Upper management eventually realized that quality suffered because of this system, so a separate position of chief inspector was created.

Between 1920 and 1940, industrial technology changed rapidly. The Bell System and Western Electric, its manufacturing arm, led the way in quality control by instituting an inspection engineering department to deal with problems created by defects in their products and lack of coordination between their departments. George Edwards and Walter Shewhart, as members of this department, provided leadership.

George Edwards stated, "Quality control exists when successive articles of commerce have their characteristics more nearly like its fellows' and more nearly approximating the designer's intent than would be the case if the application were not made. To me, any procedure, statistical or otherwise, which has the results I have just mentioned is quality control, and any procedure which does not have these results is not quality control." Edwards coined the term *quality assurance* and advocated quality as part of management's responsiblity. He said:

> This approach recognizes that good quality is not accidental and that it does not result from mere wishful thinking, that it results rather from the planned and interlocked activities of all the organizational parts of the company, that it enters into design, engineering, technical and quality planning, specification, production layouts, standards . . . and even into training . . . of administrative, supervisory, and production personnel. This approach means placing one of the officers of the company in charge of the quality control program in a position at the same level as the controller or as the other managers in the operation. Its objective would be elimination of the hunch factors that at present so largely determine the product quality of too many companies. It puts a man at the head of the quality control program in a position to establish and make effective a company-wide policy with respect to quality, to direct the actions to be taken where it is necessary and to place responsibility where it belongs in each instance.

In 1924, the mathematician Walter Shewhart introduced statistical quality control. This provided a method for economically controlling quality in mass production enviroments. Shewhart was concerned with many aspects of quality control. In his book of lectures at the Graduate School of the U.S. Department of Agriculture, he asked the reader to write several letter *A*'s as carefully as possible. He then suggested the reader observe them for variations. It was apparent that no matter how carefully one formed the letters, variations occurred. This was a simple, yet powerful example of variation in a process.

Although Shewhart's primary interest was statistical methods, he was very aware of principles of management and behavioral science. He was the first person to discuss the philosophical aspects of quality; for example, he pointed out that quality has both an objective side and a subjective side. The view that quality is multidimensional is uniquely attributable to Shewhart.

In 1935, E. S. Pearson developed British Standard 600 for acceptance sampling of incoming material. British Standard 600 was superseded by British Standard 1008, an adaptation of U.S. Z-1 Standard developed during World War II. From this point, acceptance sampling developed quickly.

World War II quickened the pace of quality technology. The need to improve product quality resulted in increased study of quality control technology and more sharing of information. In this environment, basic quality control concepts expanded rapidly. Many companies implemented vendor certification programs. Quality assurance professionals developed failure analysis techniques to solve problems; quality engineers became involved in early product design stages; and environmental performance testing of products was initiated.

In 1946, the American Society for Quality Control (ASQC) was formed. George Edwards, elected president, stated at the time, "Quality is going to assume a more and more important place alongside competition in cost and sales price, and the company which fails to work out some arrangement for securing effective quality control is bound, ultimately, to find itself faced with a kind of competition it can no longer meet successfully."

Also in 1946, Kenichi Koyanagi established the Union of Japanese Scientists and Engineers (JUSE); Ichiro Ishikawa was its first chairman. One of the first JUSE activities was to form the Quality Control Research Group (QCRG). The major members of QCRG were Shigeru Mizuno, Kaoru Ishikawa, and Tetsuichi Asaka. These three men developed and led Japanese quality control, including the birth of quality circles.

In 1950, W. Edwards Deming, a statistician who had worked at the Bell System with George Edwards and Walter Shewhart, was invited by JUSE to speak to Japan's leading industrialists. They were concerned with rebuilding Japan after the war, breaking into foreign markets, and altering Japan's reputation for producing poor quality goods. Deming convinced them that Japanese quality could become the best in the world by instituting his methods.

The industrialists took Dr. Deming's teachings to heart, and Japanese quality, productivity, and competitive position were improved and strengthened tremendously. The coveted Deming Prizes are awarded each year in Japan. One prize is awarded to an individual who shows excellent achievement in theory or application of statistical quality control, or a person who makes an outstanding contribution to the dissemination of statistical quality control techniques. Three application prizes are awarded to: (1) a company that has achieved great gains in quality, (2) a division of a company that has achieved great gains in quality, and (3) a small company for achieving great gains in quality. Prize-winning Japanese companies include Nissan, Toyota, Hitachi, and Nippon Steel. In 1989, Florida Power and Light Company became the first non-Japanese company to receive the Deming Prize.

In the 1950s and early 1960s, Armand V. Feigenbaum set out the basic principles of total quality control (TQC): quality control exists in all areas of business, from design to sales.[4,5,6] Until this time, quality efforts were primarily directed toward corrective activities, not prevention. In 1958, a Japanese quality control study team, led by Dr. Kaoru Ishikawa, visited Feigenbaum at General Electric; the team liked the name TQC and brought it back to Japan. However, Japanese TQC differs from Feigenbaum's view of TQC.[7]

The Korean War sparked increased emphasis on reliability and end-product testing. All of the additional testing did not enable firms to meet their quality and reliability objectives, so quality awareness and quality improvement programs began to emerge in manufacturing and engineering areas. Service industry quality assurance (SQA) also began to focus on the use of quality methods in hotels, banks, government, and other service systems. By the end of the 1960s, quality programs had spread throughout most of America's major corporations. American industry still enjoyed the top position in world markets, as Europe and Japan continued to rebuild.

In 1954, Dr. Joseph Juran was invited to Japan to explain to top and mid-level managers their role in the pursuit of quality control activities. Initially, Japanese managers were not interested in quality control activities, but Juran helped gain their support and commitment. Dr. Juran's visit to Japan heralded in a new era of quality control activity. He led the way from quality activities that were technologically based in factories to an overall and holistic concern for quality in all aspects of management and an organization. In one of Juran's most important books, *Managerial Breakthrough,*[8] he answers a question asked by many managers: "What am I here for?" He explains that managers have two basic functions: (1) breaking through existing processes to new levels of performance and (2) holding improved processes at their new levels of performance. These basic notions are critical to the underlying philosophy of TQC as it exists today. Another of his important books is the *Quality Control Handbook,*[9] a guide to quality improvement.

In the mid- to late 1950s, TQC was named through the work of Armand Feigenbaum, but its concepts were developed by drawing on the works of Deming and Juran. TQC expanded the concept of quality to include quality of design (including product development) and quality of performance, as well as the traditional view of quality—quality of conformance. TQC requires that all employees participate in quality improvement activities—everyone from the chairman of the board to hourly workers, from suppliers to customers, and the community.

Foreign competition began to threaten U.S. companies in the 1970s. The quality of Japanese products, such as automobiles and televisions, began to surpass American-made goods. Consumers became more sophisticated in purchase decisions and began to think of price and quality in terms of the long-term life of a product. The combination of increased consumer interest in quality and foreign competition forced American management to become more concerned with quality. The late 1970s and 1980s were marked by striving for quality in all aspects of businesses and service organizations, including finance, sales, personnel, maintenance, management, manufacturing, and service. The focus is on the entire system, not just the manufacturing line. Reduced productivity, high costs, strikes, and high unemployment caused management to turn to improvement of quality as the means to organizational survival.

Today, many organizations pursue the improvement of quality, including JUSE, ASQC (American Society for Quality Control), EOQC (European Organization for Quality Control), and IAQ (International Academy for Quality). Also, several universities have established research centers to study the improvement of quality: the University of Miami, the University of Wisconsin, the University of Tennessee, MIT Center for Advanced Engineering Study, and Fordham University. Finally, many consultants are involved in specific approaches to the improvement of quality; for example, W. Edwards Deming and his 14 points, or Joseph Juran and his managerial breakthrough, or Kaoru Ishikawa and his TQC. This book will focus on the theory of management developed by Dr. W. Edwards Deming.

DEFINITION OF QUALITY[10]

Quality is a judgment by customers or users of a product or service; it is the extent to which the customers or users feel the product or service surpasses their needs and expectations. For example, a customer who purchases an automobile has certain expectations, one of which is that the automobile engine will start when it is turned on. If the engine fails to start, the customer's expectation will not have been met, and the customer will perceive the quality of the car as poor. If an assembly line worker consistently receives usable parts in a timely manner from the worker before him on the line, his needs will be met and he will perceive the quality of those parts as good.

Quality also encompasses the never-ending improvement of a firm's *extended process*. This term refers to the expansion of the organization to include suppliers, customers, investors,

FIGURE 1–1
The Extended Process

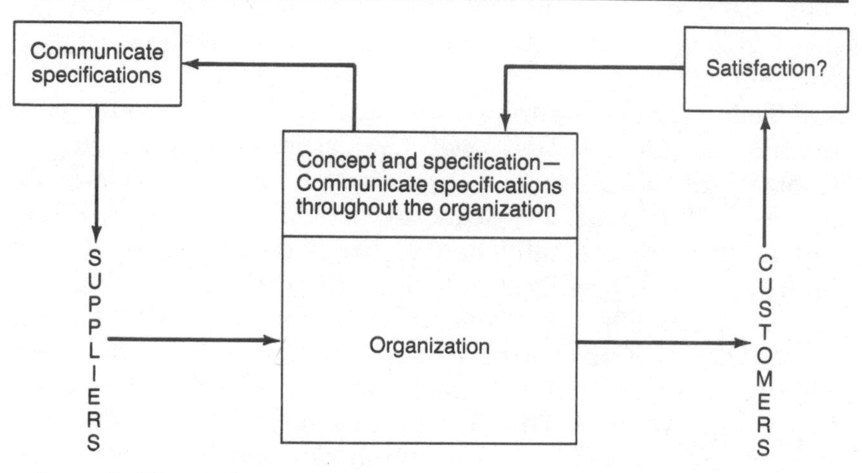

Source: H. Gitlow, S. Gitlow, A. Oppenheim, and R. Oppenheim, *Tools and Methods for the Improvement of Quality* (Homewood, Ill.: Richard D. Irwin, Inc., 1989), p. 4.

employees, and the community. Figure 1–1 illustrates the extended process.

The extended process begins with the needs of the consumer being communicated to the organization. Customer satisfaction is the ultimate goal of an organization, hence, communication of customer needs is critical to the extended process. A firm that views the customer as the most important element in the extended process must have an ongoing process to determine how its products and/or services are performing and what new specifications would improve customer satisfaction.

At the other end of the extended process are the firm's suppliers. The firm communicates the needs of its customers to its suppliers so the suppliers can help improve customer satisfaction. Firms and suppliers work together to produce quality products/services and pursue improvement of the extended process.

The concept of customers and suppliers should also be used internally in an organization. All areas and people in an organization have suppliers (areas and people up the line) and customers (areas and people down the line). Having all areas and people work with their suppliers and customers greatly enhances the pursuit of quality in the extended process.

TYPES OF QUALITY[11]

Managers must understand three types of quality if they want to improve quality in the extended process:

a. design/redesign
b. conformance
c. performance.

Quality of Design/Redesign

Quality of design begins with consumer research and service/ sales call analysis and leads to a product/service concept that meets the consumer's needs. Next, specifications are constructed for the product/service concept, as shown in Figure 1–2.

FIGURE 1–2
Quality of Design/Redesign

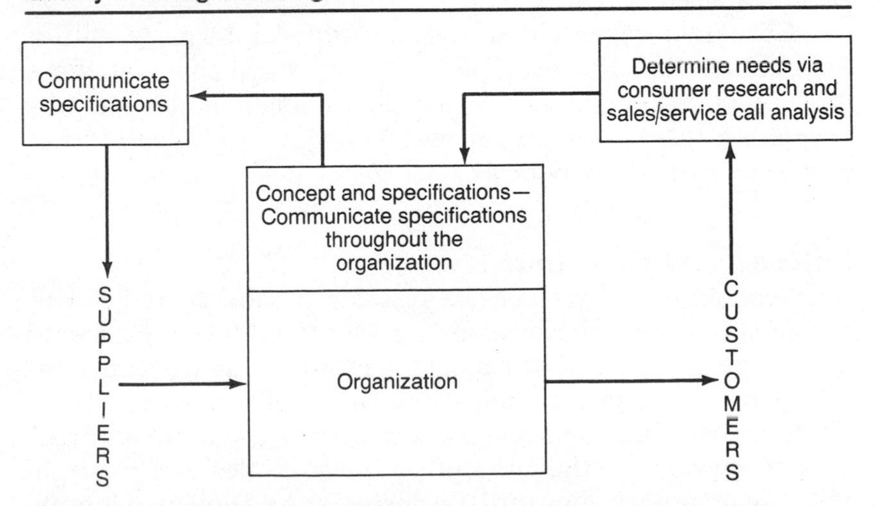

Source: H. Gitlow, S. Gitlow, A. Oppenheim, and R. Oppenheim, *Tools and Methods for the Improvement of Quality* (Homewood, Ill.: Richard D. Irwin, Inc., 1989), p. 5.

Developing a product/service concept involves establishing and nurturing an interface among marketing personnel, service personnel, and design engineering personnel. In the extended process, design engineering is one of marketing's customers and vice versa. Even in small organizations that may not have separate departments, the above interfaces are important if an organization is to continuously surpass consumer needs.

Consumer Research

Continuous and never-ending improvement of an organization's product/service concept requires ongoing consumer research and sales/service call analysis. Consumer research seeks to understand the customer's needs, both present and future. Consumer research procedures include both nonscientific and scientific studies. For example, consumer research may seek the reasons dog food purchasers buy or don't buy a particular brand. The goal of the investigation is to determine the customer's needs and redesign the dog food around those needs; for example, redesign the can size, make the can resealable, or alter the composition of the dog food. The study should be ongoing, so the firm will always be in touch with changing customer needs.

Consumer research can be performed internally within an organization. For example, employees are the customers of some management policy decisions; hence, employee surveys are a form of consumer research that could lead to improved management policy.

Sales/Service Call Analysis

Sales call analysis involves the systematic collection and evaluation of information concerning present and future customer needs that is collected during sales interactions with customers. Sales call analysis helps determine customer needs by analyzing the questions and concerns they express about products or services at the time of purchase. Sales call analysis is an important window into the customer's needs. An example of sales call analysis is a formal investigation into salesperson-customer interactions at a personal computer distributorship. The purpose of the investigation could be to collect information about the questions customers most frequently ask so the selling protocol could be modified and improved.

Service call analysis is the systematic investigation into the problems customers/users have with the performance of the product/service. Service call analysis indicates which product/service features must be changed to surpass the customer's present and future needs. An example of service call analysis is Sony Corporation's formal collection of information from field repairmen concerning customer problems with 1990 Sony KV 1920 television sets. The basic source document for the service call analysis data is the service ticket, which indicates the problem and the work done to solve it. Over time, this information would indicate problems that could require specification changes; for example, redesigning the television tuner or reducing the time between customer request for service and the completed service call.

Service call analysis can also be performed internally in an organization. For example, an area supervisor may examine the problems the next operation encounters using the parts/service forms his area delivers to the next operation. This analysis may determine what the supervisor must do to pursue process improvement within his own area.

Continuous consumer research and sales/service call analysis to aid product/services design or redesign is the goal of quality of design studies.

Quality of Conformance

Quality of conformance is the extent to which a firm and its suppliers surpass the design specifications required to serve the needs of the customer, as illustrated in Figure 1–3.

Once product/service specifications are determined via quality of design studies, the organization must continuously strive to surpass those specifications so customers receive products/services that perform properly the first time and every time during the product/service's life cycle. The ultimate goal of process improvement efforts is to create products/ser-

FIGURE 1–3
Quality of Conformance

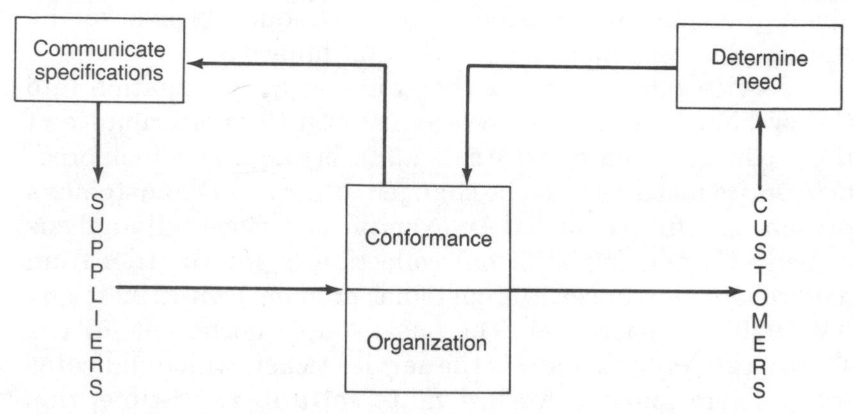

Source: H. Gitlow, S. Gitlow, A. Oppenheim, and R. Oppenheim, *Tools and Methods for the Improvement of Quality* (Homewood, Ill.: Richard D. Irwin, Inc., 1989), p. 7.

vices whose quality is so high that consumers (both external and internal) brag about them.

Some readers may question why specifications should be surpassed, rather than met.[12,13] A loss is associated with products that conform to specifications but deviate from the nominal, or target, value. Figure 1–4 shows the traditional view of losses arising from deviations from nominal. Losses are zero until the specification limit is reached, and suddenly they become positive and constant, regardless of the size of the deviation from nominal. Figure 1–5 shows a more realistic loss function. Losses begin to accrue as soon as products deviate from nominal. The view represented in this figure requires the never-ending reduction of process variation around nominal (that is, surpassing specifications) to be maximally cost-efficient and provide the degree of customer satisfaction demanded in today's marketplace.

Quality of Performance

Through consumer research and sales/service call analysis, quality of performance determines how the firm's products or services are performing in the marketplace, as shown in

FIGURE 1–4
Traditional View of Losses Arising from Deviations from Nominal

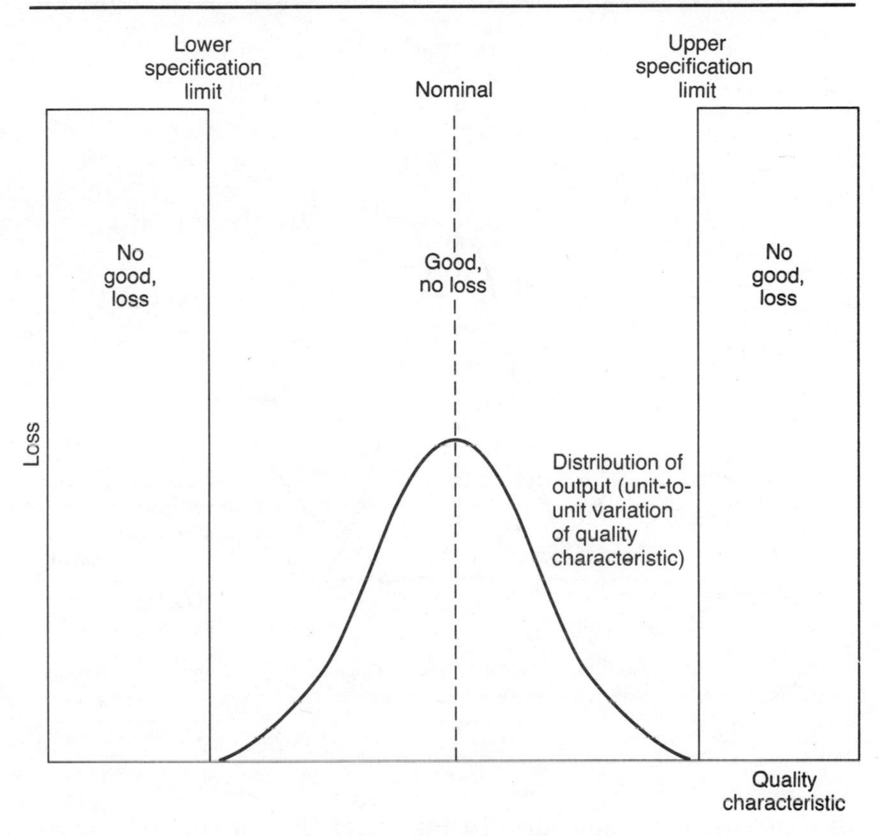

Source: H. Gitlow, S. Gitlow, A. Oppeneheim, and R. Oppenheim, *Tools and Methods for the Improvement of Quality* (Homewood, Ill.: Richard D. Irwin, Inc., 1989), p. 7.

Figure 1–6. It includes after-sales service, maintenance, reliability, logistical support, as well as why consumers do not purchase the company's products/services.

The continual flow of information generated by quality of performance studies clears the fog that exists between consumer research and sales/service call analysis and the construction of product/service/job specifications. Design engineers must work with marketing people, for example, to determine the specifications (product/service characteristics)

FIGURE 1–5
Realistic View of Losses Arising from Deviations from Nominal

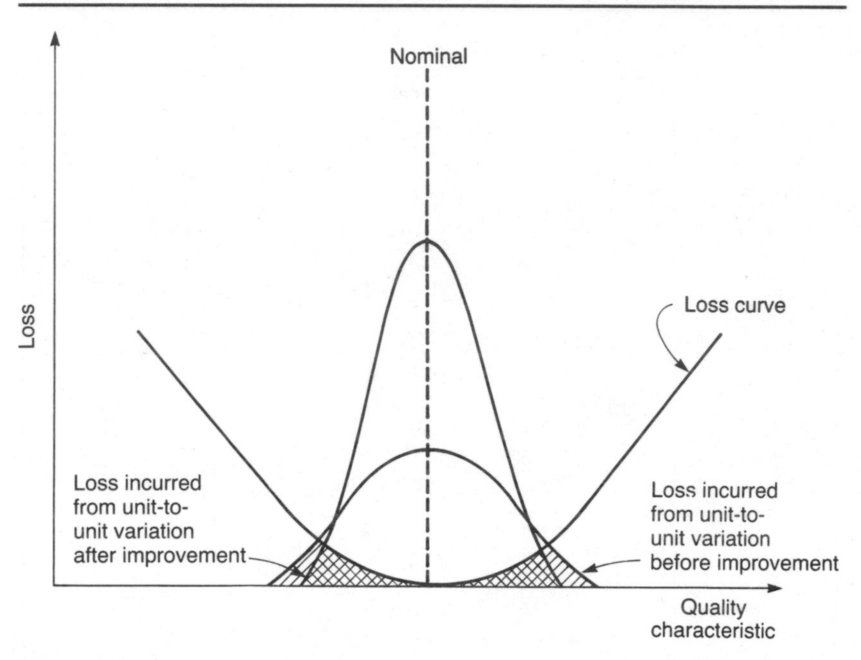

Source: H. Gitlow, S. Gitlow, A. Oppenheim, and R. Oppenheim, *Tools and Methods for the Improvement of Quality* (Homewood, Ill.: Richard D. Irwin, Inc., 1989), p. 7.

for a product/service concept that affect the consumer's satisfaction.

Once these characteristics are known and operationally defined,[14] consumers can be grouped into market segments in accordance with their desired product/service characteristics (features). Product/service characteristics and price determine if a consumer will enter a market segment; hence, product/service characteristics and price determine market size. A consumer's decision to repurchase or brag about a product/service is based on the consumer's experience with the product/service; that is, the product/service's consistent and uniform performance. Consistent and uniform performance determines the success of a product/service within a market segment;

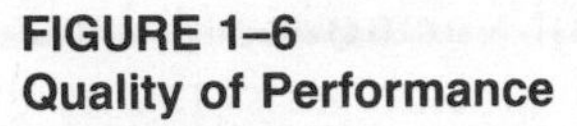

FIGURE 1–6
Quality of Performance

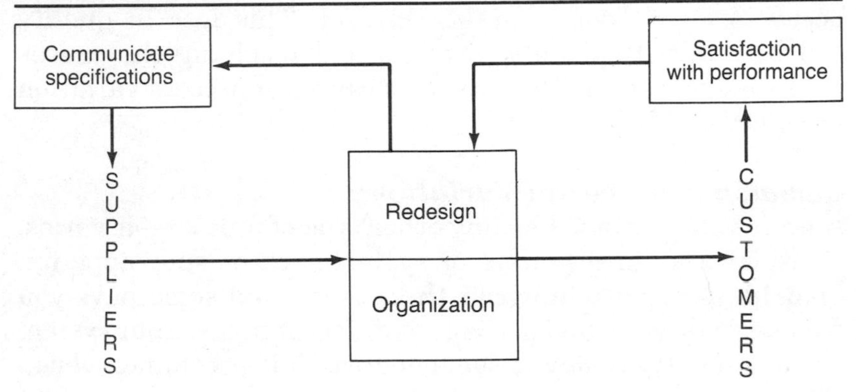

Source: H. Gitlow, S. Gitlow, A. Oppenheim, and R. Oppenheim, *Tools and Methods for the Improvement of Quality* (Homewood, Ill.: Richard D. Irwin, Inc., 1989), p. 7.

therefore, consistent and uniform performance determines market share within a market segment.

Sources of Loss in Quality

A quality of performance study should detect two sources of loss in quality. First, a loss in quality occurs when a process generates products or services whose quality characteristics package (specifications) deviates from the needs of the individual (or group of individuals) in a market segment. This loss can be remedied by increasing the number of market segments and tailoring the product to the consumer's requirements; for example, increase the number of "nominal" settings. For example, shirt neck sizes may be marketed in tenths of an inch rather than in half inches, or Velcro may be used in shirt collars instead of buttons. This segmentation strategy minimizes the loss in quality caused when the nominal levels of a product's quality characteristic package deviate from the needs of an individual (or group of individuals) in a market segment.

Second, a loss in quality also results when a process generates goods or services whose quality characteristics are not uniform (that is, there is high unit-to-unit variation). A lack of uniformity causes a product to fail to function as it is supposed to for a given market segment. This loss in quality can be reduced by understanding and resolving the causes of process variation. The two basic causes of process variation are discussed below.

Common and Special Variation[15]

A process in a firm is like any other type of process—it varies. Consider a natural process or system such as your appetite. Some days you are hungrier than usual, and some days you eat less than usual and perhaps at different times. Your system varies from day to day to some degree. This is common variation. However, if you go on a diet or become ill, you might drastically alter your eating habits for a time. This is a special cause of variation because it would have been caused by a change in the system. If you hadn't gone on a diet or become ill, your system would have continued on its former path of common variation.

Understanding the difference between common and special variation in a system is a critical element of Dr. Deming's theory of management. Management must realize that unless the system is changed (which only management can do), the system's process capability will remain the same. This capability will include the common variation inherent in any system.

Workers should not be held accountable for or penalized for common variation. Common variation could be caused by such things as poor lighting, lack of ongoing job skills training, or poor product design. Special variation could be caused by new raw materials, a broken die, or a new operator. Workers can become involved in creating and utilizing statistical methods so common and special variations can be differentiated, special variations resolved, and process improvements implemented. Because variation produces more defective and less uniform products, managers must understand how to reduce and control variation. Understanding and controlling variation leads to improvement of quality.

Managers must balance the cost of having many market segments with the benefits of high consumer satisfaction caused by small deviations between an individual consumer's needs and the product characteristic package for the market segment. Also, managers must continually strive to reduce variation in product characteristics for all market segments.

These two sources of loss in quality must be detected in the quality of performance stage of the extended process. This information is then fed back into the quality of design stage and quality of conformance stage of the extended process.

IMPROVEMENT AND INNOVATION (QUALITY CREATION)

Improvement and innovation are both required if a firm is to be competitive in the future. Process improvement modifies current products and processes to continuously reduce the difference between customer needs and process performance. Tools such as consumer research and service/sales call analysis help in this endeavor.

The purpose of innovation is twofold: (1) to create a dramatic breakthrough in decreasing the difference between customer needs and process performance, and (2) to discover the customer's future needs. Ideas for innovation regarding the customer's future needs cannot come from direct queries to customers; rather, they must come from the producer.

Asking customers what they want can only help producers improve existing products or services; it cannot help producers anticipate the customer's future needs.[16] Consumers do not know what innovations they will want in the future; for example, a consumer could not tell you he wants a facsimile machine or an automatic loading camera before such things existed. These types of breakthroughs must be discovered by the producer studying the problems customers have when using products and services and not by asking customers what they want in the future.

For example, in 1974, the camera market was saturated with cameras that satisfied customers' current needs—cameras were reliable, relatively inexpensive to use, and gave good pictures. This created a nightmare for the camera industry. Canon asked consumers: "What more would you like in a camera?" Consumers replied they were satisfied with their cameras. In response, Canon studied negatives at film processing laboratories and discovered the first few pictures on many rolls were overexposed, indicating users had difficulty loading cameras. This presented an opportunity to innovate camera technology. The customer could not have been expected to think of this innovation. In response, Canon developed the automatic loading camera. This is an excellent example of innovation of a current product or service. The same type of procedure could have been used to discover consumer needs for a new product or service.

THE RELATIONSHIP BETWEEN QUALITY AND PRODUCTIVITY[17]

Why should organizations try to improve quality? If a firm wants to increase its profits, why not raise productivity? The following example demonstrates the folly of this thinking. The Universal Company produces 100 widgets per hour. Of these 100 units, 20 percent are defective. This has been the rate of production and the rate of defects for the past 10 years. The board of directors now demands that top management increase productivity by 20 percent. The directive goes out to the employees, who are told that, instead of producing 100 widgets per hour, the company must produce 120. The responsibility for producing more widgets falls on the employees, creating stress, frustration, and fear. They try to meet the new demands but must cut corners to do so. The pressure to raise productivity creates a defect rate of 25 percent and only increases production to 104 units, yielding 78 good widgets, less than the original 80, as shown in Figure 1–7a.

Stressing productivity often yields the opposite of what management desires. The following example demonstrates a new way of looking at productivity and quality.

The Dynamic Factory produces 100 widgets per hour with 20 percent defective. Top management is continually trying to improve quality, thereby increasing productivity. Top man-

FIGURE 1–7a
Productivity versus Quality Approach to Improvement—Universal Company Output

	Universal Company Output	
	Before Demand for 20% Productivity Increase	*After Demand for 20% Productivity Increase*
	(Defect rate = 20%)	(Defect rate = 25%)
Widgets produced	100	104*
Widgets defective	20	26
Good widgets	80	78

* Only reached 104, not required 120, but defect rate rose from 20 percent to 25 percent. More widgets were produced; but more were defective, yielding less productivity.

Source: H. Gitlow, S. Gitlow, A. Oppenheim, and R. Oppenheim, *Tools and Methods for the Improvement of Quality* (Homewood, Ill.: Richard D. Irwin, Inc., 1989), p. 13.

agement realizes Dynamic is making 20 percent defectives, which translates into 20 percent of the total cost being spent to make bad units. If Dynamic's managers can improve the process, they can transfer resources from the production of defectives to the manufacture of additional good products. Management makes some changes, at no additional cost, so only 10 percent of the output is defective. This increases productivity, as shown in Figure 1–7b. Management's ability to improve the process resulted in a decrease in defectives, yielding an increase in good units, quality, and productivity.

Benefits of Improving Quality

Stressing quality to increase productivity results in the following benefits:

1. Productivity rises (in the Dynamic Factory example, from 80 good units in the 100 produced to 90 good units in the 100 produced).
2. Quality improves (from 80 percent good units to 90 percent good units).

FIGURE 1–7b
Productivity versus Quality Approach to Improvement—Dynamic Factory Output

Dynamic Factory Output			
	Before Improvement		*After Improvement*
	(Defect rate = 20%)		(Defect rate = 10%)
Units produced	100	→	100
Units defective	20	Process	10
Good units	80	Improvement	90
		→	

Source: H. Gitlow, S. Gitlow, A. Oppenheim, and R. Oppenheim, *Tools and Methods for the Improvement of Quality* (Homewood, Ill.: Richard D. Irwin, Inc., 1989), p. 13.

3. Cost per good unit is lowered.
4. Price can be cut.
5. Workers' morale goes up because they are not seen as the problem, which will lead to further benefits:
   - Less employee absence.
   - Less burnout.
   - More interest in the job.
   - Motivation to improve work.

Stressing only productivity will sacrifice quality and may even lower output. Employee morale will plunge, costs will rise, customers will be unhappy, and stockholders will be concerned. Stressing quality can yield all the desired results: less rework, greater productivity, lower unit cost, price flexibility, improved competitive position, increased demand, larger profits, more jobs, and more secure jobs. Customers get high quality at a low price; vendors get predictable long-term sources of business; and investors get profits. Everybody wins.

THE QUALITY ENVIRONMENT

Improving quality is highly dependent on management's ability to create an atmosphere that demonstrates its commitment to understanding quality and to accepting responsibility for improving it. The "quality environment" encourages teamwork, communication, joint problem-solving, trust, security, pride of workmanship, and never-ending improvement. A true cooperative spirit prevails in this type of atmosphere. Teamwork is a prerequisite for the firm to function and to constantly improve the extended process.

In the quality environment, the corporate culture changes so workers are no longer afraid to point out problems in the system. Management is actively involved with the workers in the never-ending improvement of the extended process. Workers and management learn to cooperate on teams and to speak the language of statistics and process control. Workers are responsible for communicating to management the information they have about the system, so management can act. Never-ending improvement of the process eventually leads to higher quality, reduced costs, and greater profitability. Never-ending improvement of the process refers to all aspects of the extended process, not just within the organization. This includes working with vendors, customers, the community, investors, and the board of directors.

FOURTEEN POINTS FOR MANAGING NEVER-ENDING IMPROVEMENT OF THE EXTENDED PROCESS[18]

Dr. W. Edwards Deming operationalized his theory of management in his "Fourteen Points." Understanding and acceptance of the Fourteen Points lead to a commitment by management and provide a framework for action. A brief overview of the Fourteen Points will give the reader a theoretical basis for planning for quality. The reader is referred to Deming's *Out of the Crisis*[19] for a full discussion of Deming's theory of management for improving quality, productivity, and competitive position. Other references include: Gitlow and Gitlow, *The Deming Guide to Quality and Competitive Position*[20]; Scherkenbach, *The Deming Route to Quality and Productivity: Road Maps and Roadblocks*[21]; and Walton, *The Deming Management Method.*[22]

Deming's theory of management incorporates the use of

statistical tools and behavioral techniques. Gitlow, Gitlow, Oppenheim, and Oppenheim, *Tools and Methods for the Improvement of Quality,*[23] gives a detailed discussion of the statistical tools and Scholtes, *The Team Handbook,*[24] provides a detailed discussion of the behavioral techniques. Both are important when planning for quality because they help create a corporate climate focused on nurturing process uniformity and creating process improvement. Planning is not possible in organizational cultures without a quality focus and chaotic and/or high process variability.

Although the points are presented separately and can create improvement individually, the synergistic implementation of all of the points will improve quality in a never-ending fashion. The Fourteen Points are listed below and are followed by a brief discussion of each point.

1. Create constancy of purpose toward improvement of product and service, with the aim to become competitive and to stay in business and to provide jobs.
2. Adopt the new philosophy. We are in a new economic age. Western management must awaken to the challenge, must learn their responsibilities, and take on leadership for change.
3. Cease dependence on inspection to achieve quality. Eliminate the need for inspection on a mass basis by building quality into the product in the first place.
4. End the practice of awarding business on the basis of price tag. Instead, minimize total cost. Move toward a single supplier for any one item, on a long-term relationship of loyalty and trust.
5. Improve constantly and forever the system of production and service, to improve quality and productivity, and thus constantly decrease costs.
6. Institute training on the job.
7. Institute leadership (see point 12). The aim of leadership should be to help people and machines and gadgets to do a better job. Leadership of management is in need of overhaul, as well as leadership of production workers.
8. Drive out fear, so that everyone may work effectively for the company.
9. Break down barriers between departments. People in research, design, sales, and production must work as a team

to foresee problems of production and in use that may be encountered with the product or service.

10. Eliminate slogans, exhortations, and targets for the work force asking for zero defects and new levels of productivity.

11a. Eliminate work standards (quotas) on the factory floor. Substitute leadership.

11b. Eliminate management by objectives. Eliminate management by numbers, numerical goals. Substitute leadership.

12a. Remove barriers that rob the hourly worker of his or her right to pride of workmanship. The responsibility of supervisors must be changed from sheer numbers to quality.

12b. Remove barriers that rob people in management and in engineering of their right to pride of workmanship. This means "inter alia," abolishment of the annual or merit rating and of management by objective, management by the numbers.

13. Institute a vigorous program of education and self-improvement.

14. Put everybody in the company to work to accomplish the transformation. The transformation is everybody's job.

Point 1: Create constancy of purpose toward improvement of product and service, with the aim to become competitive and to stay in business and provide jobs.

Long-term perspective and constancy of purpose are necessary ingredients for the never-ending improvement of the extended process. An organization's mission statement, operating philosophy, and objectives should provide a framework for consistent action on a day-to-day and long-term basis. Concern for improvement and innovation of products and processes (the problems of today and tomorrow) gives management the foresight to allocate resources to become competitive, stay in business, and provide jobs.

Establishing a mission statement is synonymous with setting a process's nominal or target average level. Establishing a plan so all employees (management, salaried, and hourly), members of the board of directors, and shareholders can interpret the mission statement uniformly and pursue it is a problem of reduction of variation.[25]

Creating an environment that encourages everyone in the extended process to innovate and cooperate on continually improving quality and surpassing customers' needs will create (1) increased productivity, (2) better competitive position, (3) satisfactory return for stockholders, (4) secure employment, and (5) continued existence.

Point 2: Adopt the new philosophy. We are in a new economic age. Western management must awaken to the challenge, must learn their responsibilities, and take on leadership for change.

Adopting the new philosophy means creating an environment in which everybody is a winner. This means altering the corporate culture from a competitive environment to a cooperative environment. In a cooperative environment, everybody wins. The customer wins products and services he or she can brag about and rejects commonly accepted levels of defects, rework, shoddy workmanship, and poor service. The firm wins returns for investors and secure jobs for employees. Suppliers win long-term customers for their products. The community wins an excellent corporate citizen.

The costs to all members of the extended process from a win-lose mentality are unknown and unknowable, but they are huge. These costs include rework, waste and redundancy, material, manpower, capital equipment, facility space, warranty, retesting, reinspection, shipping, customer dissatisfaction, schedule disruptions, and destruction of the individual. Accepting a win-lose mentality has eroded America's competitive position in world markets.

Top management must be committed to nurturing an "I win-you win" mentality of business and life.[26] Top management can do several things to promote the "I win-you win" mentality in the extended process.

First, top management can expand its organizational vision to include all members of the extended process: customers, suppliers, employees, investors, and the community. This vision must simultaneously consider and balance the needs of all members of the extended process (see point 1).

Second, top management must step out of line to the point of exile among its peers to create the "I win-you win" mentality in the extended process (see point 14).

Third, top management must stop its obsession with overcontrol, such as management by objectives or variance analysis in cost accounting (more on this in point 11b). Overcontrol, an extremely destructive form of management, increases variability in the extended process and makes prediction and planning almost impossible. Instead, top management should study and acquire knowledge that explains what it must do to stop overcontrolling (tampering) the components of the extended process.

Fourth, top management must learn and manage in accordance with a theory of management. Top management must give up the narcotic of "the illusion being realistic" as the guiding force behind its actions and start managing on the basis of a theory of management; that is, the theory behind the Fourteen Points. A requirement for understanding the Fourteen Points is possessing a system of "profound knowledge," as Deming has defined below.[27]

1. Knowledge for study of variation. Variation there will always be, between people, output in service, and of product. What is the variation trying to tell us?
2. Knowledge of variation helps us to understand the losses of tampering. There are two mistakes.
   a. Treating a fault, complaint, mistake, accident, as if it came from a special cause when actually it came from a common cause.
   b. The converse.
3. Knowledge of procedures aimed at minimum economic loss from these two mistakes (see Shewhart control charts).
4. Knowledge about interaction of forces; effects of the system on the performance of people; dependence, inter-dependence between people, groups, divisions, companies, countries.
5. Knowledge about losses from decisions of management made in the absence of knowledge of variation. Losses from demands that lie beyond the capability of the system (e.g., MBO). Losses from quotas. Losses from suboptimization.
6. Knowledge about the production of chaos and loss that results from successive application of random forces that may be individually unimportant. Examples are:
   - Worker training worker.
   - Executives working together on policy without guidance of profound knowledge.
   - Committees and government agencies working without guidance of profound knowledge.

8. Knowledge about losses from competition for share of market. Losses from barriers to trade.
9. Some knowledge about the theory of extreme values.
10. Some knowledge about the statistical theory of failure.
11. Theory of knowledge:
    a. Any plan, however simple, requires prediction.
    b. There is no knowledge without theory.
    c. There is no knowledge without prediction.
    d. Experience teaches nothing unless studied with the aid of theory.
    e. An example teaches nothing unless studied with the aid of theory.
    f. Operational definition: communication.
    g. No number of examples establishes a theory.
    h. There is no true value of anything.
    i. There is no such thing as a fact. Any two people have different ideas about what to record about what happened.
12. Knowledge of psychology.
    - Intrinsic motivation (for innovation, for improvement, for joy in work, for joy in learning).
    - Extrinsic motivation (humiliating, a day's pay for a day's work).
    - Overjustification: reward for an act or achievement that brought happiness to the doer, for the sheer pleasure of doing it. The result of the reward is to throttle repetition. He will never do it again.
13. People learn in different ways and at different speeds.
14. Necessity for transformation (government, industry, education) to leadership within the company; elimination of competition, ranking people, grades in school, and prizes for athletics in school.
15. Knowledge about the psychology of change.

Finally, top management must use its power (formal, knowledge, and personality) to create and nurture the I win-you win cooperative view of business and life.

Point 3: Cease dependence on inspection to achieve quality. Eliminate the need for inspection on a mass basis by building quality into the product in the first place.

Mass inspection is essentially checking goods with no consideration of how to make them better, improve the process, or achieve higher quality. Some people believe that if product inspections were carried out properly, quality would improve. In reality, inspection neither improves nor guarantees quality. Mass inspection at any stage in the extended process does not make a clean separation of good from bad. Mass inspection is too late. Quality is not improved by after-the-fact inspection; the defective items have already been produced.

One problem with 100 percent inspection is inaccuracy. Play the role of inspector for a few moments and count the number of *f*'s in the following passage:

FINISHED FILES ARE THE RESULT
OF YEARS OF SCIENTIFIC STUDY COMBINED
WITH THE EXPERIENCE OF MANY YEARS.

Did you find six *f*'s? When this exercise is done in a group, more than one third of the participants typically come up with the wrong answer. This demonstrates the fallibility of 100 percent inspection.

Deming advocates a plan that minimizes the total cost of incoming materials and final product. The rule simply states inspect all or none. Statistical evidence of quality is its base. The rule for minimizing the total cost of incoming materials and final product is referred to as the kp rule,[28] and it specifies when all items should be inspected and when none should be inspected.

The kp rule facilitates the collection of process or product data such that variation can be continually reduced. This occurs when process data are collected with variables control charts and when estimates of the fraction of out-of-specification material are calculated in a process capability study.

Defect detection depends on mass inspection to sort conforming from defective material. Dependence on mass inspection does not decrease variation. Further, inspection does not create a uniform product within specification limits. Rather, product is bunched around specification limits, or at best, product is distributed within specification limits with large variance and tails cut off at the specification limits.

Defect prevention can only reduce variation such that

products are within specification. Unfortunately, entropy will result in a process that operates just within specification limits, eventually going out of specification limits. Further, defect prevention gives employees the impression that their jobs, with respect to the reduction of variation, are accomplished if they achieve "zero defects." This creates an atmosphere of laxness, which will ultimately take its toll.

Never-ending improvement works at continuously reducing variation within specification limits. Traditional loss functions, where loss is zero until a specification limit is reached and then becomes positive and constant, are not adequate for today's marketplace. Rather, a loss function should be used that demonstrates the economic wisdom of continuous reduction of variation, as shown in Figure 1–5.[29]

Point 4: End the practice of awarding business on the basis of price tag. Instead, minimize total cost. Move toward a single supplier for any one item on a long-term relationship of loyalty and trust.

Many organizations purchase solely on the basis of price, without an adequate measure of quality. Purchasing agents are encumbered by a managerial policy that dictates buying from the low bidder as standard operating procedure. Without an adequate measure of quality, however, price is meaningless, as the following example demonstrates.

Three vendors submit bids to a firm for a large quantity of a certain part. Vendor A charges $12 per unit. Vendor B charges $11 per unit, and Vendor C charges $10 per unit. If the purchasing agent considers only the price tag, then Vendor C will get the contract. However, if the purchasing agent considers quality and price, another vendor might get the contract.

Let's say Vendor A has been pursuing never-ending improvement of quality. He has improved his production process so only one unit per million is defective. Consequently, the effective price the firm would pay for A's good product is:

$$\frac{\$12}{(1 - 0.000001)} = \$12 \text{ per unit.}$$

Vendor B has also been pursuing process improvement using statistical process control, but not as long as Vendor

A. He has reduced his average defect rate to 10 percent. The 10 percent figure has been stable over some time. The effective price the firm would pay for B's good product is:

$$\frac{\$11}{(1-0.10)} = \$12.22 \text{ per unit.}$$

Vendor A is the better buy. However, both vendors have the organizational capacity to improve because they are in control of their processes, even if Vendor B is temporarily at a disadvantage.

Vendor C has no records showing the capability of his process to produce a good product. Therefore, the effective price the firm would pay for C's good product is unknown:

$$\frac{\$10}{(1-?)} = \text{Unknown per unit.}$$

It is likely that Vendor C's defect rate is higher than A's or B's because his process is not in control. Vendor C's material may get prohibitively expensive if you consider the costs of using nonconforming material and the subsequent rework. Vendor A's price becomes more attractive because total cost includes the purchase cost plus the cost to put the material into production.

The purchasing agent must be able to judge quality, which necessitates education in statistics and process control. The agent must also understand the problems encountered with purchased materials as they move through the extended process. Purchasing agents interact with other employees, customers, and vendors and have to develop the skills to determine satisfaction or dissatisfaction and feed this information back into the process of never-ending improvement.

Deming also stresses the need to move toward single-source suppliers, instead of maintaining multiple sources for each item purchased. Quality is promoted by encouraging long-term single-source relationships between buyers and vendors that are based on statistical evidence of quality. In single-source relationships based on trust, vendors are willing to modify their processes to meet revised quality of design specifications and work with buyers to incorporate customer feedback into improving their processes. This type of relationship allows for open negotiation of the contract to meet the needs of the buyer and vendor and, ultimately, the customer.

Purchasing can be continuously improved through the never-ending reduction of variation in purchasing procedures, incoming materials, number of suppliers for any given item, and number of purchasing agents for any given item.[30]

A one-time purchase from a supplier can be made without regard to the supplier's process. However, this is not true for continuing purchases over time. For continuing purchases, continuous reduction of variation in the supplier's process is critical. Long-term relationships with a supplier make sense if the supplier consistently meets the organization's needs and will continue to improve its ability to do so in the long run.

Multiple supplier processes, each of which has small variations, combine to create a process with large variation. This means an increase in the variablity of inputs to the organization, which is counter to the reduction of variation. Consequently, reducing the supply base from many suppliers to one supplier is a rational action. This idea applies to both external and internal suppliers.

Point 5: Improve constantly and forever the system of production and service, to improve quality and productivity, and thus constantly decrease costs.

Management is responsible for the entire system and for all of its various processes. This responsibility includes the design of the product or service, the measurement of the amount of trouble with the product or service, and the assignment of responsibility for action to remove the cause of the problem.

Process and product improvement and innovation are accomplished by planning projects that require statistical and behavioral methods used by everyone in an organization. Although planning projects is very important to never-ending improvement, implementation must be gradual. First, the organization's environment should demonstrate the new commitment to quality, a long-term perspective, and a growing trust between management and labor. This gradual process generally takes a year or more. Statistical and behavioral training are necessary for *all* employees, including management and hourly employees. Additionally, individuals involved in project planning should receive training in planning tools and techniques, the focus of this book.

The Deming cycle[31] can help management reduce the difference between the customer's needs and process performance. It is a derivative of the scientific method aimed at processes. The Deming cycle was originally called the Shewhart cycle after its founder, W. A. Shewhart. In 1950, the Japanese renamed it the Deming cycle.

The Deming cycle is composed of four basic stages: a "plan" stage, a "do" stage, a "study" stage, and an "act" stage. Hence, the Deming cycle is sometimes referred to as the PDSA cycle (*P*lan-*D*o-*S*tudy-*A*ct cycle). A plan is developed (Plan); the plan is tested on a small scale or trial basis (Do); the effects of the plan are studied (Study); and appropriate corrective actions are taken (Act). These corrective actions can lead to a new or modified plan, and so the PDSA cycle continues forever in an uphill cycle of never-ending improvement. The Deming (PDSA) cycle is shown in Figure 1–8.

FIGURE 1–8
The Deming (PDSA) Cycle

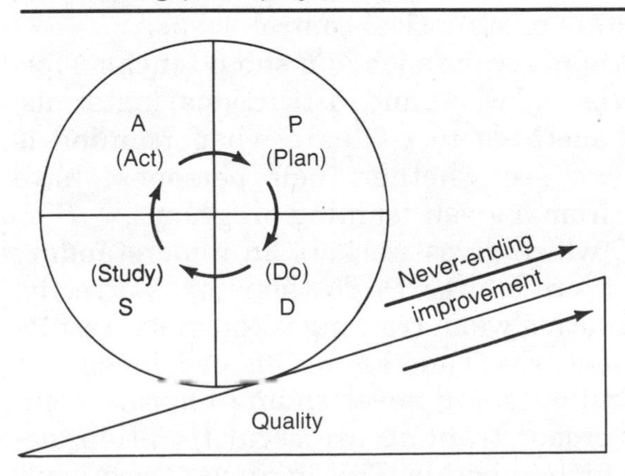

Source: Adapted from H. Gitlow, S. Gitlow, A. Oppenheim, and R. Oppenheim, *Tools and Methods for the Improvement of Quality* (Homewood, Ill.: Richard D. Irwin, Inc., 1989), p. 160.

Point 6: Institute training on the job.

Job skills training is an ongoing, integrated approach to employee growth and development. Employees are the most important asset of an organization, and the company's long-term commitment to them includes proper job skills training. People need training in how to perform their jobs, where the job is broadly defined to include an understanding of the organization's product or service and the quality characteristics associated with that product or service. Employees must understand operational definitions, specifications, interactions between process and product quality characteristics, and the extended process.

Everyone in an organization should similarly be trained in basic statistical methods, and the organization should foster everyone's ability to understand variation. Statistical methods and statistical thinking create a uniform way for employees to view the organization's processes. This focuses attention on the causes of variation and points to methods to remove those causes, reduce variation in a process, and create improvement in the organization. Statistical methods and statistical thinking allow management to separate systems problems, for which only they are accountable, from special problems that can be dealt with by all employees.

Further, employees should be trained using statistical methods that indicate their training is complete by showing when they reach a state of statistical control.

Training is part of everyone's job and should include formal class work, experiential work, and instructional materials. By using statistical methods to evaluate when training is complete, trainers can see whether their personnel have learned all they can from a given training program.

Proper training, which gives workers an understanding of their jobs, specific procedures to do their jobs correctly, and a method of evaluating when training is complete, results in quality improvement. Everyone knows his or her job and is in statistical control pursuing never-ending improvement. Further benefits of proper training are security, pride, decrease in stress, and higher morale. This improves the organizational climate and promotes better working relationships.

Point 7: Institute leadership (see point 12). The aim of leadership should be to help people and machines and gadgets to do a better job. Leadership of management is in need of overhaul, as well as leadership of production workers.

"In place of judgment of people, rating them, putting them into slots (outstanding, excellent, on down to unsatisfactory), there will be leadership, see point 12b. The aim of leadership is to help people, to improve the service and profits of a company."[32]

Some of Deming's attributes of a leader are listed below.[33]

1. A leader understands how the work of his group fits the aims of the company. The purpose of this group is to support these aims.
2. He works in cooperation with preceding stages and with following stages toward optimization of the efforts of all stages. He sees his group as a link in a system.
3. He tries to create for everybody interest and challenge and joy in work. He tries to optimize the education, skills, and abilities of everyone, and helps everyone to improve. Improvement and innovations are his aim.
4. He is coach and counsel, not a judge.
5. His source of power is: (1) formal, (2) knowledge, (3) personality. A successful leader develops 2 and 3 and does not rely on 1. He has nevertheless obligation to use number 1, as this source of power enables him to change the system—equipment, material, methods—to bring improvement, such as to reduce variation in output.
6. He uses plots of points and statistical calculation with knowledge of variation to try to understand the performance of himself and of his people. One aim is to try to learn how he himself can improve his leadership. Another aim is to learn who if anybody is outside the system. Simple rearrangement of the work might be the answer. Transfer to another job may require prudence and tact, as the man to be transferred may interpret this as one way to get rid of him.
7. He creates trust. He creates freedom and innovation. He is aware that creation of trust requires that he take a risk.[34]

8. He does not expect perfection.
9. He listens and learns without passing judgment on him that he listens to.
10. He understands the benefits of cooperation and the losses from competition.[35]

Point 8: Drive out fear, so that everyone may work effectively for the company.

Fear in organizations has a profound impact on those working in the organization and on the functioning of the organization. On an individual level, fear can cause physical and physiological disorders, such as a rise in blood pressure or an increase in heart rate. Behavior changes, emotional problems, and physical ailments are often the result of fear and stress generated in work situations, as are drug and alcohol abuse, absenteeism, and burnout. These maladies affect any organization. An employee working in a climate of fear experiences poor morale, poor productivity, stifling of creativity, reluctance to take risks, poor interpersonal relationships, and reduced motivation to work for the best interests of the company. The economic loss to the company is immeasurable.

Management is obliged to ensure the physical and emotional health of its employees for their well-being and that of the organization. Many managers use their power to create fear because they believe the way to motivate employees is through coercive power. Workers believe they will be punished if they do not perform. This generates fear, which impedes their performance and is counterproductive.

Fear emanates from lack of job security, possibility of physical harm, ignorance of company goals, shortcomings in hiring and training, poor supervision, lack of operational definitions, failure to meet quotas, blame for the problems of the system, and faulty inspection procedures. Management has control over these elements and is responsible for changing the organizational climate. Driving out fear is significant in creating the quality environment. Fearful, anxious employees cannot participate in improving quality and productivity.

Fear creates variability between an individual's or team's actions and the actions required to surpass the customer's needs and wants. In a fear-filled environment, a system of statistically based management will not work because people in the system will view statistics as vehicles for policing and judging, rather than as vehicles for providing opportunities for improvement.

Point 9: Break down barriers between departments. People in research, design, sales, and production must work as a team to foresee problems of production and in use that may be encountered with the product or service.

Barriers exist in organizations; this is a fact of corporate life. Organizations are not created with barriers: team spirit, unity, and cooperation are the initial cries of a newly formed company. However, these attitudes quickly disappear as people's roles become functional and as communication problems, competition, and fears arise. Barriers impede the smooth flow of the extended process, and everyone suffers, most notably the customer. Rework and costs are increased, and quality and customer satisfaction are decreased.

Barriers exist in many places within the extended process. Competition, personal grudges, different views of a problem, and different priorities all lead to barriers between departments or areas within departments. Barriers also exist between levels in the hierarchy. Poor communication between employees and supervisors, supervisors and middle managers, and middle and upper management is common. There are also barriers between the firm and its vendors, the firm and its customers, union and management, and the firm and the community.

Barriers between departments cause multiple interpretations of a given message. This increases variability in the actions taken with respect to a given message. Operational definitions create a common language for communication between departments and consequently reduce variability in the actions taken on processes and products by different departments. "Operationally defining the ultimate customer's needs and expectations so that everyone understands how he contributes to the success of the organization is a solid step to breaking down barriers between departments."[36]

Breaking down barriers involves changing attitudes so

employees identify with, and cooperate in pursuing, the organization's unifying goals instead of specialized department goals; this is called *social memory*.[37] Social memory facilitates employees from different departments supporting each other by allowing them to give up current departmental resources to another department in greater need of these resources for the overall good of the organization. Social memory dictates that the donating department's sacrifices will be remembered in future allocation cycles.

Open communication and confronting the barriers are the first steps to developing social memory in an organization. Creating teams can help to develop social memory and destroy departmental barriers; teams can be created either within or across departmental lines. Training in teamwork is critical.

Point 10: Eliminate slogans, exhortations, and targets for the work force asking for zero defects and new levels of productivity.

Setting targets for people has become common. It is believed that having a target will motivate the individual to achieve and will clarify what is expected of that person. Unfortunately, it usually has the opposite effect. Generally, targets are set arbitrarily by someone for someone else, as in the case of a sales manager asking for a 5 percent increase in sales from the sales force. If that sales manager does not provide new methods or means to achieve the target, then it is a meaningless plea. Examples of slogans, posters, and targets that do not help anyone do a better job are:

- Do it right the first time.
- Safety is job one.
- Increase return on net assets 3 percent next year.
- Decrease costs 10 percent next year.

"Zero defects" is a misleading slogan/target. According to Deming, "Zero defects, meet specifications, incoming and outgoing, are not good enough. Of course, we wish not to violate specifications, but to meet specifications is not enough. The pieces in an assembly must work together. Assemblies must work together."[38] Just meeting specifications will not guarantee customer satisfaction.

The kinds of targets listed above do not represent action

statements for employees, but rather, management's wishes for a desired result. When employees are measured against goals they do not know how to achieve and are judged by management that will punish them for not achieving the desired results, they are filled with tension, fear, and resentment. This is far different from management's objective of motivating people. If management wants to motivate people by hanging up posters, the emphasis should be on the progress management is making in never-ending improvement. Statistical methods that demonstrate this are appropriate mechanisms for communicating management's commitment to the new philosophy.

The system and its variation are the responsibility of management. Targets, slogans, and posters try to shift that responsibility to the employee. For example, a sign in a factory reading "Safety is better than compensation!" is attempting to shift the burden for safety from factory management to the worker. Assigning blame and punishment to an individual for problems beyond his or her control is a cruel and inhuman form of management.

Point 11a: Eliminate work standards (quotas) on the factory floor. Substitute leadership.

Work standards, measured day work, and piecework are names given to an industry practice that has devastating effects on American quality, productivity, and competitive position. A work standard is a specified level of performance determined by someone other than the worker who is actually performing the task. Work standards and quotas consider only quantity, not quality, so they are at odds with the new philosophy.

The effects of setting quotas, in general, are negative. They do not provide a road map for improvement, and they prohibit good supervision and training. In a quota system, workers are blamed for problems that are beyond their control. Workers are encouraged to produce defectives to meet the quota. This has dire consequences. Workers are robbed of their pride. Employees want to produce high-quality goods and to feel positively about themselves and their jobs, but management won't let them.

Quotas set too high or too low produce additional devastating effects. Setting too-high quotas increases pressure on workers and results in production of more defectives. Worker morale and motivation are diminished because the system encourages the making of defectives. The effects of too-low quotas are also destructive. Workers who have met their quota spend the last hour of the day doing nothing; their morale is also destroyed.

Work standards are negotiated values that have no bearing on a process or its capability. Changes in the process's capability are not considered, so the standards do not reflect the potential of the current system. They create variability in performance by obscuring an employee's understanding of the job. Work standards create fears that undermine the smooth operation of the workplace and create an undesirable atmosphere contrary to the Deming philosophy.

Work standards are also a cap on improvement. Once the standard is reached, employees stop working in fear of a new and higher standard. Thus, work standards create variability between actual performance and desired performance.

If a work standard is between a system's upper natural limit (UNL) and lower natural limit (LNL), the standard can possibly be met, but meeting the standard this way is simply a random lottery. If a work standard is above the UNL of the system, then there is little chance the standard will be met unless management changes the system. Rather than focusing on the standard as a means to productivity, management should focus on stabilizing and improving the process to increase productivity.

Work standards are frequently used for budgeting, planning, and scheduling, and they provide invalid information for management decisions. Planning, budgeting, and scheduling would improve greatly if they were based on the process's capability as determined by statistical methods.

The alternative to using work standards and quotas on the factory floor to direct workers is to institute leadership, as discussed in point 7.

Point 11b: Eliminate management by objectives. Eliminate management by numbers, numerical goals. Substitute leadership.

Management by objectives, management by numbers, and

management by numerical goals are just sophisticated methods to legitimize the managerial use of arbitrary numerical goals to hold people accountable for the problems of the system and, consequently, to steal their humanity and pride of workmanship. Management by objectives typifies the evils of management by numbers and management by numerical goals.

Managers use management by objectives to systematically break the grand plan into smaller and smaller subsections, which are then assigned to an individual or group to achieve. This is considered fair because the subsection goals emerge out of a negotiation between supervisor and supervisee. For example, an employee may negotiate a 3 percent increase in output instead of a 3.5 percent increase, as long as the subsection's goals equal those of the "master plan." The employee is not being given any new tools, resources, or methods to achieve the 3 percent increase, so he or she must scavenge from the existing system to meet the goals. Also, the request from management to increase 3 percent is arbitrary. Why not increase 20 percent or 50 percent? The expectation of increases is absurd unless management makes changes in the system.[39]

The alternative to using management by objectives, management by numbers, or management by numerical goals to direct subordinates is to institute leadership as discussed in point 7.

Point 12a: Remove barriers that rob the hourly worker of his right to pride of workmanship. The responsibility of supervisors must be changed from sheer numbers to quality.

Many organizations in the United States do not use workers to their fullest potential, robbing them of their pride of workmanship and treating them as commodities. This loss of pride is an obstacle to achieving competitive advantage. Pride provides the impetus to perform better and to improve quality for the worker's self-esteem, for the company, and for the customer. People enjoy taking pride in their work, but very few are able to do so because of poor management. Managers don't pay enough attention to people and their problems, so employees become disenfranchised, instead of being involved and utilized to their maximum potential.

Several factors contribute to the loss of pride of workmanship; for example, if employees don't understand the company's mission and what is expected of them to achieve that mission, and hence are confused and do not identify with the organization; if employees are forced to act as automatons, unable to think or use their skills; if employees are blamed for the problems of the system. Hastily designed products and inadequately tested prototypes translate into production of low-quality merchandise. Everyone in the organization suffers a loss of pride because everyone is associated with making "junk." Inadequate supervision and training prohibit pride of workmanship because they foster fear and incompetence and encourage production of defectives. Faulty equipment, materials, and methods hinder workers in the performance of their jobs and lessen positive feelings about their work and the organization.

No matter what the source of loss of pride in workmanship, organizations will reap tremendous benefits if they help employees reclaim pride in their work. Maximizing the potential of the work force and creating loyalty, excitement, interest, and team cooperation are extremely important to never-ending improvement.

Some quality experts have started to equate the concepts of pride in workmanship and joy in work. Consequently, point 12 could be restated as "Remove barriers that rob employees of their joy in work." Joy in work for employees can be extended to include: joy in products and services for customers, joy in healthy returns for investors, joy in buyers of output for suppliers, and joy in economic and social health for the community. This expansive concept of joy defines an "I win-you win" situation for all members of the extended process.

Some examples of barriers to pride in workmanship can be found in Gitlow and Gitlow, *The Deming Guide to Quality and Competitive Position.*

Point 12b: Remove barriers that rob people in management and in engineering of their right to pride of workmanship. This means "inter alia," abolishment of the annual or merit rating and of management by objective, management by the numbers.

The annual or merit rating system robs people in management of their right to pride of workmanship. First, it destroys teamwork by encouraging every person and every department to focus on individual goals, rather than on the organization's goals, to obtain a positive rating in the annual review. This leads to serious suboptimization. Simultaneous seeking of different, and possibly conflicting, goals creates variability in management's behavior, which creates confusion and fear as to what everybody's job is. This destroys the employee's ability to take pride in his or her workmanship. By eliminating the annual review, it becomes feasible to focus everyone's attention on the organization's goals.

Second, the annual review reduces initiative or risk-taking because once an objective is reached, effort stops. This is counter to the notion of continuous and never-ending improvement. This robs the employee of the ability to take pride in his or her workmanship by denying the employee the joy of continuous improvement.

Third, the annual review can cause an employee to lower planned performance level to increase the chances of meeting objectives. This robs the employee of the ability to take pride in workmanship by preventing him or her from reaching toward his or her potential.

Fourth, the annual review can foster banking of performance to create a cushion for the next annual review cycle. This banking makes the employee a liar and steals his or her ability to take pride in his or her workmanship.

Fifth, the annual review can increase variability in employee performance, resulting from actions such as rewarding everyone who is above average and penalizing everyone who is below average. In this type of situation, employees who are below average try to emulate employees who are above average. However, because the employees who are above average and those who are below average are part of the same system (only common variation is present), those who are below average are adjusting their behavior based on common variation. This steals the employees' right to pride in workmanship because it causes confusion with respect to the appropriate response an employee should make to process conditions.

Sixth, the annual review assumes people are directly and solely responsible for their output. This assumption fails to consider the distinction between the effect of the individual and the effect of the system on output. It fails to appreciate the causes of variation and that most of the variation in performance can be attributed to the system, not the individual. The system is the responsibility of management. The shifting of blame for system problems from process owners to subordinates is one of the largest root causes of loss of pride in workmanship.

Seventh, the annual review focuses on the short term. A short-term focus promotes frustration and fear for employees because it decreases their ability to work toward long-term improvement and innovation. This frustration and fear decreases the employee's ability to take pride in workmanship.

An Alternative to the Annual Review or Merit System. Instead of the annual review or merit system, management can control and improve development of group objectives (intradepartmental objectives, as opposed to interdepartmental objectives, that can be resolved by the department) through the reduction of variation.[40]

Variation in the pursuit of departmental objectives can be reduced by operationally defining *group objectives*. Once group objectives are defined, people from different departments can adopt the same group objectives because everyone participated in their development. This reduces the variability caused by employees seeking different departmental objectives.

The *process* of developing group objectives focuses group attention on the sources of variation and the actions required to reduce that variation. Suppliers should meet with customers to determine which process or product characteristics they can provide to surpass the customer's needs. Once customers and suppliers agree on the desired process or product characteristic, they can determine the possible areas, or sources, of improvement to satisfy customer needs. This can be accomplished, for example, by constructing a cause-and-effect diagram that indicates sources of variability in the characteristics requiring improvement and the possible resources to be used for reducing that variation.

Next, it is important to determine which departments, and which employees within those departments, can effect the necessary improvement. Once the appropriate individuals have been identified, they should form a group to develop mutual objectives that will lead to the desired improvement, which in turn will result in customer satisfaction.[41]

Improvement of the group objectives process requires an understanding of the sources of variability that can affect group objectives. Once these sources of variability have been isolated, they must be eliminated to create an organization that can form group objectives consistently and efficiently. This can happen only when the *inputs* to the group objective process are stable with a low level of variability; for example, when manpower does not vary with respect to objectives (individuals are all focused on the organization's objectives); when materials do not vary with respect to characteristics; when methods have been operationally defined and improved with statistical guidance; when machinery is managed on statistical signal; and when the environment creates uniformity in behavior.[42]

A Proposal that Fosters Consistency. Management must understand variation to recognize whether an employee is or is not operating in the system. An employee can exist in only one of three categories: in the system, out of the system on the negative side, and out of the system on the positive side. The latter two categories signify the employee is in need of special attention. For example, if an employee shows improving or deteriorating performance for more than seven periods in a row, that can be used as evidence that the employee needs special attention. This illustrates institution of modern methods of supervision.

If all employees are within the system, then to reward or punish employees on the basis of performance (or merit) would be destructive because the punished employees will try to emulate the rewarded employees when there is no difference between the two types of employees—they are both in the system and any difference is due to common variation, which is out of the individual's control. This type of reward/punish management will increase the variation between employees. In this situation, any improvement must be a result of improvements in the system, which will benefit all employees.

If one or more employees are not within the system (special employees), then management must determine: (1) if the special employees form their own special system and (2) if the rest of the employees are within the old system. Next, management must determine the sources of variation for the special employees and use this information to reduce variation and create consistency and improvement.[43]

Point 13: Institute a vigorous program of education and self-development.

Education and self-development are important vehicles for continuously improving employees, both professionally and personally. Education in chemistry, physics, accounting, and law, to name a few areas, will help employees better understand their jobs and, consequently, enable employees to improve their jobs. Education in consensus decision-making, conflict resolution, team building, psychology, and time management will help employees' interpersonal skills, both professionally and personally. Education in Deming's theory of management is the first step for an organization that wants to improve quality. Everyone in the organization should receive this education, beginning with top management. Statistical education at all levels is also necessary to prepare employees to implement these methods.

As an organization improves, it will free up resources that can be used for the education and self-development of its employees. These improvements will result in less variability in processes, products, and jobs, continuing the never-ending cycle of improvement.

Point 14: Put everybody in the company to work to accomplish the transformation. The transformation is everybody's job.

Top management in an organization has to make a commitment to transform the organization. Setting the change process in motion involves the recognition that problems exist and a desire to create a new organizational environment, one in which the never-ending improvement of quality is the primary goal. Top management has to begin by creating a critical mass of people in the organization who understand the philosophy and want to change the corporate culture. Organizing for quality involves planning and establishing administrative structures that promote quality.

THE MESSAGE BEHIND THE FOURTEEN POINTS[44]

Dr. Deming's message to managers is to stop focusing on the judgment of results from processes and to start focusing on the improvement of the processes that created the results. Dr. Deming's Fourteen Points can be classified in light of management's focus, as shown in Figure 1–9.

Dr. Deming's message to managers, if internalized, will enable them to pursue the never-ending improvement of a process through the acquisition of process knowledge in an environment created by living the Fourteen Points. This pursuit is used to develop an ability to predict the future, making possible planning for the improvement of quality or for other noble endeavors (even, for example, improvement of the human condition).

Dr. Deming's message leads to the reduction of variation, which ignites a chain reaction—reduced variation leads to reduced rework, increased quality, decreased unit cost, increased productivity, increased price flexibility, increased competitive advantage, increased profit, more jobs, and more secure jobs. Deming's message to managers improves their ability to predict the future and to plan. This ability is based on the following notions: (1) variation is natural, (2) two types of variation, common and special, may exist in any process, (3) process identity depends on eliminating special variation, and (4) process improvement depends on reducing common variation, centering a process on nominal, operational definitions, and understanding interactions between process variables. The value of these abilities extends beyond the pursuit of quality. These abilities create opportunities to gain process knowledge and to predict on the part of a process expert in any field of endeavor.

FIGURE 1–9
The Fourteen Points and Management Focus

Title for Group of Points	*Start Focusing on Improvement of the Process*	*Stop Focusing on Judgment of Results*
Purpose	1. Create constancy of purpose 14. Put everybody to work to accomplish the transformation	
Leadership	7. Institute leadership	11. Eliminate numeric goals and quotas 12. Remove barriers to pride of work 8. Drive out fear
Cooperation	2. Adopt the new philosophy	9. Break down barriers between departments 4. End the practice of awarding business on the basis of price alone
Training and education	6. Institute training on the job 13. Institute a vigorous program of education and self-improvement	
Improvement of processes	5. Improve constantly and forever the system of production and service	3. Cease dependence on inspection to achieve quality 10. Eliminate slogans and exhortations

CHAPTER SUMMARY

Issues of quality have existed since tribal chiefs, kings, and pharaohs ruled. The modern history of quality is marked by great advances between 1920 and the 1950s by George Edwards, Walter Shewhart, W. Edwards Deming, Armand Feigenbaum, and Joseph Juran. The 1970s and 80s have been characterized by foreign competition threatening American companies. A renewed emphasis on quality control has been the response, and W. Edwards Deming, Joseph Juran, and Armand Feigenbaum are among the leaders in this area. This book focuses on the philosophy and methods of W. Edwards Deming.

Quality is defined as a judgment by customers or users of a product or service. It also encompasses the never-ending improvement of a firm's extended process, or the internal processes of an organization, along with those processes associated with customers, suppliers, investors, employees, and the community. Three types of quality, design/redesign, conformance, and performance, are integral to improvement of the extended process.

Top management is responsible for the never-ending improvement of quality and must understand the three types of quality, the relationship between quality and productivity, and the benefits of improving quality. The quality environment of a firm is critical and stresses teamwork and communication. Deming's Fourteen Points for management provide a guide to creating and establishing the quality environment through behavorial change and the use of statistical methods to continually improve the process. The Fourteen Points focus management attention away from judging past results and toward improving and innovating processes for the future. This book presents some tools for planning that facilitate process and product improvement and innovation in organizations pursuing Dr. Deming's theory of management.

ENDNOTES

1. H. J. Harrington, "Quality's Footprints in Time," *IBM Technical Report,* September 20, 1983, pp. 2–12.
2. W. A. Golomski, "Quality Control—History in the Making," *Quality Progress,* July 1976.
3. Paraphrased from H. Gitlow, S. Gitlow, A. Oppenheim, and

R. Oppenheim, *Tools and Methods for the Improvement of Quality* (Homewood, Ill.: Richard D. Irwin, Inc., 1989), pp. 8–12.

4. A. V. Feigenbaum, "Total Quality Control," *Harvard Business Review,* November 1956.
5. A. Feigenbaum, "The Challenge of Total Quality Control," *Industrial Quality Control* 13, no. 11, (May 1957), p. 17.
6. A. Feigenbaum, *Total Quality Control,* (New York: McGraw-Hill, 1961).
7. See K. Ishikawa, *What Is Quality Control? The Japanese Way* (Englewood Cliffs, N.J.: Prentice-Hall, 1985), pp. 90–91.
8. J. Juran, *Managerial Breakthrough* (New York: McGraw-Hill, 1964).
9. J. Juran et al., *Quality Control Handbook* (New York: McGraw-Hill, 1951, 1962, 1974, 1988).
10. Paraphrased from Gitlow, Gitlow, Oppenheim, and Oppenheim, *Tools and Methods for the Improvement of Quality,* pp. 1–8.
11. Ibid.
12. Ibid, pp. 164–67.
13. G. Taguchi and Y. Wu, *Off-Line Quality Control* (Nagoya, Japan: Central Japan Quality Control Association, 1980), pp. 7–9.
14. A characteristic is operationally defined if it is stated in terms of a criterion, a test, and a decision so people can communicate over its value.
15. H. Gitlow and S. Gitlow, *The Deming Guide to Quality and Competitive Position* (Englewood Cliffs, N.J.: Prentice-Hall, 1987), pp. 9–10.
16. Paraphrased from a lecture by Dr. W. E. Deming concerning managerial education in the United States at Fordham University, November 6, 1989.
17. See Gitlow, Gitlow, Oppenheim, and Oppenheim, *Tools and Methods for the Improvement of Quality,* pp. 12–14.
18. Modified from ibid. and Gitlow and Gitlow, *The Deming Guide to Quality.*
19. W. E. Deming, *Out of the Crisis* (Cambridge, Mass.: MIT, Center for Advanced Engineering Study, 1986).
20. Gitlow and Gitlow, *The Deming Guide to Quality.*
21. W. Scherkenbach, *The Deming Route to Quality and Productivity: Road Maps and Roadblocks* (Washington, D.C.: CeePress Books, 1986).

22. M. Walton, *The Deming Management Method* (New York: Dodd, Mead, 1986).
23. Gitlow, Gitlow, Oppenheim, and Oppenheim, *Tools and Methods for the Improvement of Quality.*
24. P. Scholtes, *The Team Handbook* (Madison, Wis.: Joiner Associates Inc., 1988).
25. W. Scherkenbach, *The Deming Route to Quality and Productivity,* pp. 133–34.
26. Ideas adapted from Alfie Kohn, *No Contest: The Case Against Competition* (Boston: Houghton Mifflin, 1986), pp. 189–96.
27. Profound knowledge is defined by W. E. Deming in: W. E. Deming, *Foundation for Management of Quality in the Western World* (Osaka, Japan: Institute of Management Sciences, July 24, 1989), pp. 11–13.
28. See chapter 18 in Gitlow, Gitlow, Oppenheim, and Oppenheim, *Tools and Methods for the Improvement of Quality,* for a discussion of Deming's kp rule for minimizing the total cost of incoming materials and final product.
29. See ibid., Chapter 15, for a discussion of the Taguchi loss function.
30. Scherkenbach, *The Deming Route to Quality and Productivity,* pp. 133–36.
31. Deming, *Out of Crisis,* pp. 86–89.
32. Deming, *Foundation for Management of Quality in the Western World,* pp. 16–17.
33. Ibid.
34. Carlisle and Parker, *Beyond Negotiation* (New York: John Wiley & Sons, 1989).
35. Kohn, *No Contest.*
36. Ibid., p. 82.
37. William Ouchi, *The M-Form Society* (Reading, Mass.: Addison-Wesley Publishing, 1984), chap. 1.
38. Excerpted from a letter by W. E. Deming, titled, *Foundation for Management of Quality in the Western World,* October 10, 1989.
39. Drawn from Gitlow and Gitlow, *The Deming Guide to Quality and Competitive Position,* p. 160.
40. Scherkenbach, *The Deming Route to Quality and Productivity,* pp. 57–61.

41. Ibid., pp. 59–60.
42. Ibid., pp. 60–61.
43. Ibid., pp. 62–69.
44. Michael Tveite, "The Theory Behind the Fourteen Points: Management Focused on Improvement Instead of on Judgment," presented at the Third International Deming User's Group Conference, King's Island, Ohio, August 22, 1989.

CHAPTER 2

OVERVIEW OF QUALITY TOOLS AND METHODS

THE PDSA CYCLE

The PDSA (Shewhart) cycle can aid management in constructing and executing plans that reduce the difference between customer needs and process performance. The PDSA cycle comprises four basic stages:

1. "**P**lan" stage.
2. "**D**o" stage.
3. "**S**tudy" stage.
4. "**A**ct" stage.

A plan is developed (Plan); the plan is tested on a small scale or trial basis (Do); the effects of the trial plan are monitored (Study); and appropriate process improvements are made (Act). These improvements, called *countermeasures,* can lead to a new or revised plan, or process modifications, and so the PDSA cycle continously decreases the difference between customer needs and process performance.

The PDSA cycle operates by recognizing that problems (opportunities for improvement) in a process are determined by the difference between customer (internal and/or external) needs and process performance. A great difference may mean high customer dissatisfaction, but there is also great opportunity for improvement. A small difference may mean low customer dissatisfaction, consequently less opportunity for improvement.[1] Regardless of the extent of opportunity for improvement, continuous effort should be focused on decreasing the difference between customer needs and process performance. The four PDSA stages can accomplish this.

Stage One: Plan

Collecting data about process variables is critical when determining a plan of action for decreasing the difference between customer needs and process performance. Earlier, we discussed the three types of quality that must be understood in the never-ending improvement of the extended process. Data concerning customer needs are collected via *quality of performance* studies. These same data are evaluated and transformed into variables that may be acted upon during *quality of design* studies. Data concerning process capability are collected via *quality of conformance* studies. These process data should be collected on variables for which process improvement action can be taken.

A plan must be developed to determine the effect(s) of manipulating process variables on the difference between process performance and customer needs. The plan must be tested using *quality of design, conformance,* and *performance* studies. The tests should be conducted in a laboratory, production setting, office setting, or on a small scale with customers (both internal and external). The results of these tests will lead to a concrete plan for manipulating the process variables to decrease the difference between customer needs and process performance. This book presents and explains some useful tools and methods for developing a plan.

Stage Two: Do

The plan established in stage one is set into motion on a trial basis in the Do stage. The trial plan should be conducted in a laboratory, work setting, or on a small scale with customers, both internal and external. This stage is accomplished through a three-part process. First, the organization must educate everyone to understand the relationship between the manipulated variables and the proposed decrease in the difference between customer needs and process performance. Second, training is required so everyone understands who the plan will affect so they can modify the way they perform their jobs. After accomplishing parts one and two, the plan can be set into motion as the third part of the Do stage.

Stage Three: Study[2]

The plan, which was set into motion in stage two (Do), must be continually monitored (Study) to answer two questions. First, are the manipulated process variables decreasing the difference between customer needs and process performance? Second, are the downstream effects of the plan creating problems or improvements? The results of statistical studies in the Study stage lead to the Act stage.

Stage Four: Act

The Act stage implements the plan modifications discovered in the Study stage, further narrowing the difference between customer needs and process performance. Hence, the PDSA cycle continues forever in the never-ending improvement of the extended process.

The Act stage considers whether the manipulated process variables have diminished the difference between customer needs and process performance. If it has not been effective, the PDSA cycle returns to the Plan stage to search for other process variables that may decrease the difference. However, if the manipulation of process variables produced the desired results, then the Act stage leads back to the Plan stage to determine the optimal levels at which to set the manipulated process variables. It is important that all procedures are standardized so everyone performs a given procedure in the same way. This standardization increases communication and decreases the possibility of error.

The PDSA cycle is the basic method used to stabilize a process and continuously work toward improving the process.[3]

TOOLS AND METHODS OF THE PDSA CYCLE

The many tools and methods that can be used to decrease the difference between customer needs and process performance fall into three groups: the seven management tools, the seven basic quality control tools, and the advanced quality control tools. Seven, the number of tools in two categories, is considered to be a lucky number in Japan, where many of these tools were popularized. Seven represents the minimum number of pieces of equipment a samurai warrior must have to go to battle, as shown in Figures 2–1a and 2–1b.

The Seven Management Tools

The first group of tools and methods are useful to managers in their planning efforts (see Plan in the PDSA cycle). The seven management tools include:

1. Affinity diagrams.
2. Interrelationship digraphs.
3. Systematic diagrams.
4. Matrix diagrams.
5. Matrix data analysis.
6. PDPC analysis.
7. Arrow diagrams.

These will be discussed extensively later. A brief description of each follows.

Affinity Diagram

An affinity diagram uses a brainstorming procedure to help a team gather and organize large amounts of creative input (ideas, fact, opinions) about a product or process problem. Figure 2–2 shows the organized output, called an affinity diagram, from a team brainstorming session about "What do we do to accomplish a move successfully?" The team's view of the key issues involved in a successful move are:

1. Checking out.
2. Planning.

FIGURE 2–1a
Samurai with Seven Tools

Source: Noriaki Kano, "Problem Solving Activities," University of Miami Quality Program Visiting Lecture Series, October 25, 1988, p. 3.

FIGURE 2–1b
Nanatsu Dohgu (Seven Tools)

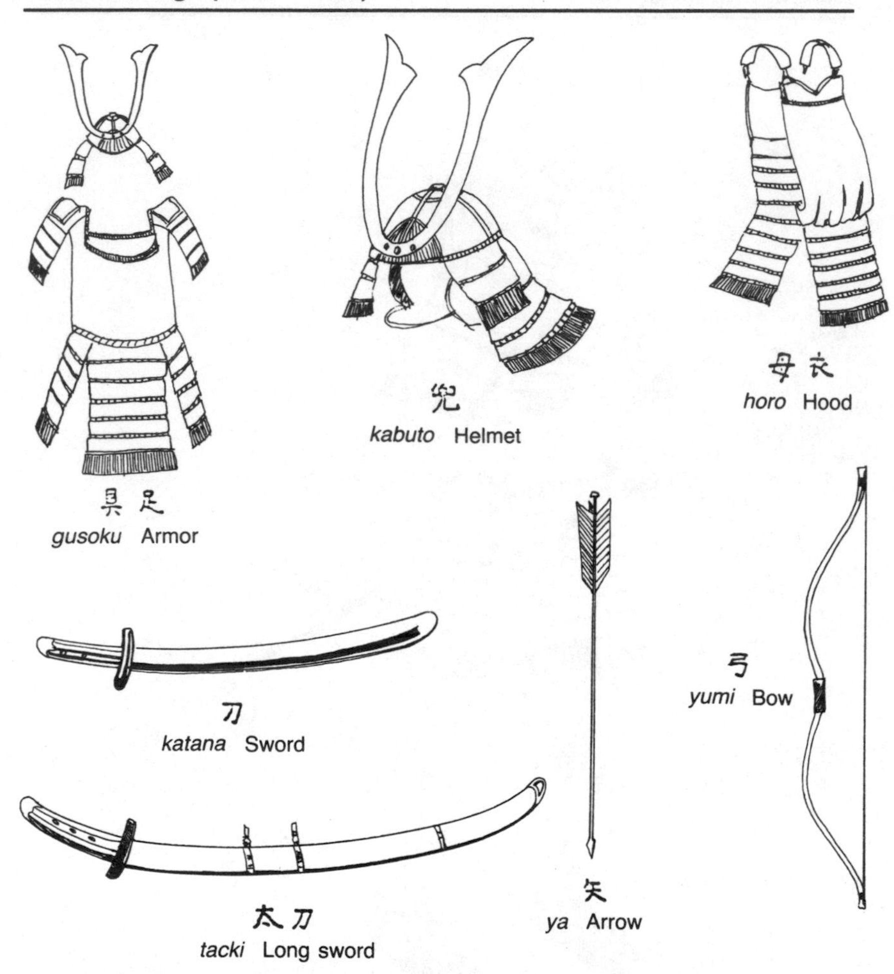

Tools kept always at hand. Originally, the seven weapons which a Samurai carried with himself when he went to the battlefield: armor, sword, long sword, bow, arrow, hood, and helmet.

Source: Noriaki Kano, "Problem Solving Activities," University of Miami Quality Program Visiting Lecture Series, October 25, 1988, p. 4.

3. Unpacking.
4. Packing.
5. Settling in.
6. Checking in.
7. Social concerns.
8. New purchases.
9. Drive.
10. Get damage deposit back.

A detailed study of the above 10 categories, and the detail behind each category, will help the team understand the issues surrounding a successful move to a new location.

Interrelationship Diagraph

An interrelationship diagraph (diagram/graph) is used to understand problems that have complex cause-and-effect relationships and/or complex objective-to-means relationships. Frequently, the input for an interrelationship diagraph is the output of an affinity diagram. Figure 2–3 shows an interrelationship diagraph that helps a team understand the cause-and-effect relationships between the latent issues determined in the affinity diagram in Figure 2–2 about a successful move to a new location. The interrelationship diagraph shows the "planning" issue affects more issues than any other issue with respect to a successful move (it is a root cause); consequently, planning must be addressed first to move successfully.

Systematic Diagram

A systematic diagram helps determine the actions required to improve process or product performance. Figure 2–4 shows part of the results of a team effort to determine the actions and subactions required to plan for a successful move to a new location. The actions are:

1. Packing.
2. Unpacking.
3. Checking in.
4. Checking out.
5. Social concerns.

FIGURE 2–2
Example of Affinity Diagram

Problem Statement: What do we do to accomplish a move successfully?

Purpose: To gather and organize large amounts of creative input (ideas, opinions, thoughts, etc.) about a product or process problem.

Example:

CHECKING OUT
- Close bank accounts
- Disconnect phone service
- Forward mail
- Change address w/ mags, credit cards, etc.
- Call utility companies to disconnect service
- Send out change of address cards to friends/family

PLANNING
- Choose best route to get to new apt.
- Where to stay first night?
- Rent U-Haul or moving van company?
- Friends to help
- Hold a rummage sale?
- Assign responsibility in family
- Choose date to move out/in

UNPACKING
- Decide which room to unpack first
- Arrange, rearrange furniture
- Assemble bed
- Unpack
- Find places for everything
- Wash dishes
- Clean new apt.
- Hang pictures

PACKING
- Mark boxes contents
- Pack belongings
- Get boxes and packing material
- Eat, pack, or toss old groceries
- Throw out stuff you don't want to move
- Load truck

SETTLING IN
- Find new cleaners / hair place, gym, etc.
- Find closest grocery store
- Select new school, visit new school, register
- Drive new route to work
- Open new bank account
- Find new church
- Get referrals for new doctors

CHECKING IN
- Pick up new keys
- Deposits on new utilities
- Call utility companies to connect new service
- Make deposit on new property
- Get new phone, phone number

SOCIAL CONCERNS
- Have good-bye party
- Have housewarming party
- Buy beer, pizza for helpers

NEW PURCHASES
- What do you need to buy for new place?
- Buy food for new place

DRIVE

GET DAMAGE DEPOSIT BACK
- Clean the old property
- Repair damage
- Give keys to old landlord
- Have landlord check

FIGURE 2–3
Example of Interrelationship Diagraph

Problem
Statement: What do we do to accomplish a move successfully?

Purpose: To organize and identify major cause-and-effect relationships of elements of a problem. Input for the I.D. can come from the affinity diagram.

Example:

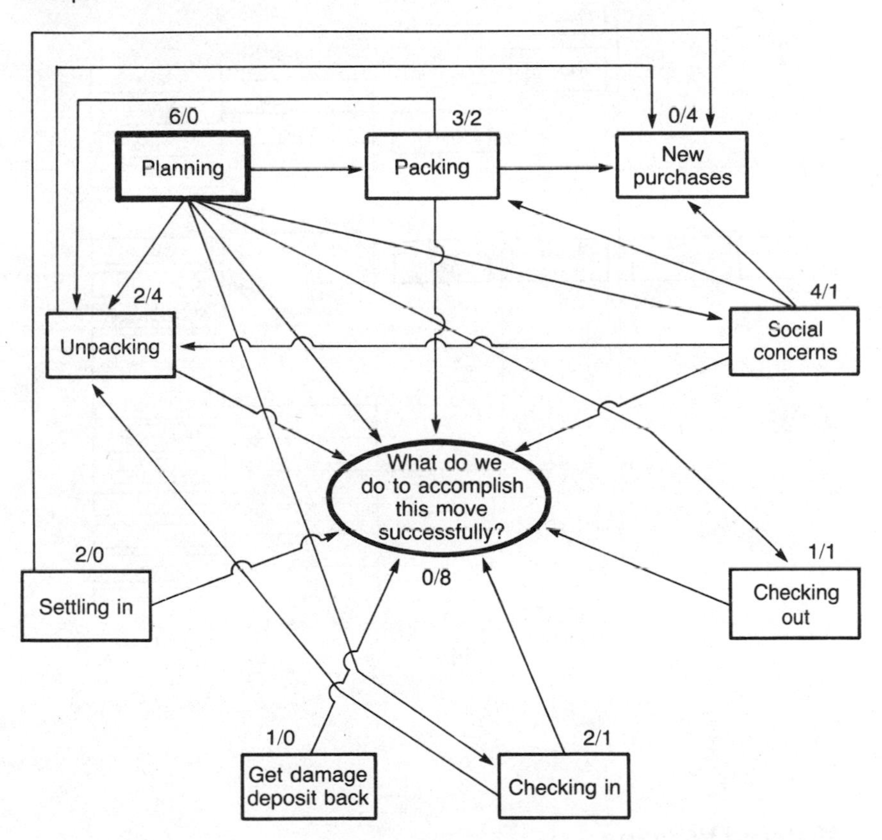

The actions to the right of "planning" were taken from the interrelationship diagraph in Figure 2–3. The subactions to the right of the actions come from the individual cards in the affinity diagram shown in Figure 2–2 and from additional brainstorming.

FIGURE 2–4
Example of Systematic Diagram

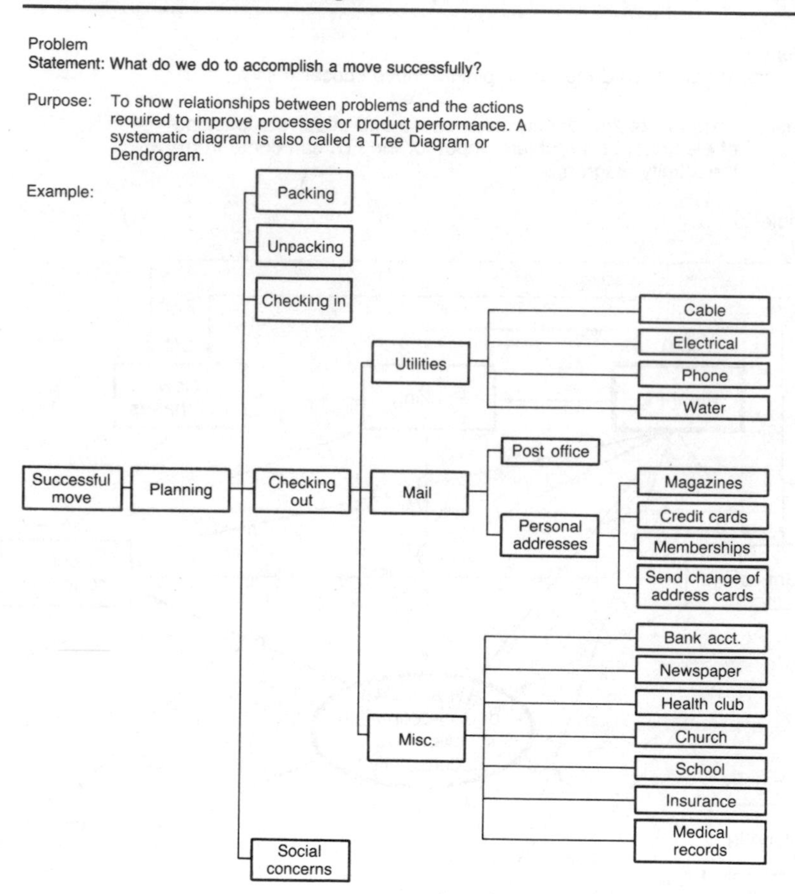

Matrix Diagram

A matrix diagram shows the interrelationships between two or more process or product characteristics. Frequently, a matrix diagram is used to portray the actions required for a process or product improvement versus the people/areas responsible to carry through said process or product improvements. Figure 2–5 shows a matrix diagram being used to

FIGURE 2–5
Example of Matrix Diagram

Problem
Statement: Who is responsible for the components of the move?

Purpose: To build on the systematic diagram by identifying actions required and the people/areas responsible to carry out the actions.

Example:

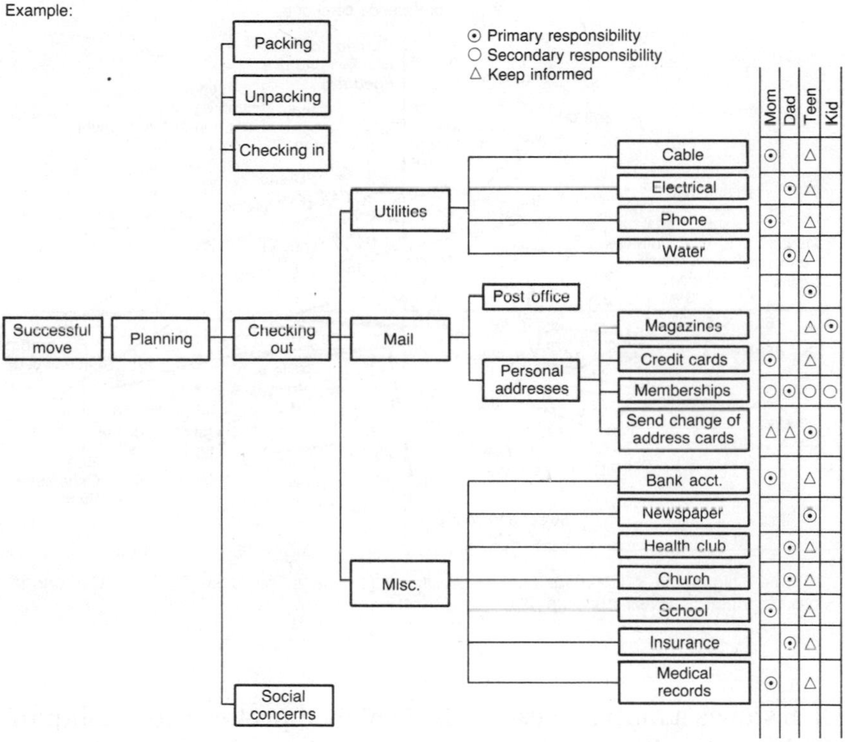

⊙ Primary responsibility
○ Secondary responsibility
△ Keep informed

- Successful move
  - Planning
    - Packing
    - Unpacking
    - Checking in
    - Checking out
      - Utilities
        - Cable
        - Electrical
        - Phone
        - Water
      - Mail
        - Post office
        - Personal addresses
          - Magazines
          - Credit cards
          - Memberships
          - Send change of address cards
      - Misc.
        - Bank acct.
        - Newspaper
        - Health club
        - Church
        - School
        - Insurance
        - Medical records
    - Social concerns

	Mom	Dad	Teen	Kid
Cable	⊙		△	
Electrical		⊙	△	
Phone	⊙		△	
Water		⊙	△	
Post office			⊙	
Magazines			△	⊙
Credit cards	⊙		△	
Memberships	○	⊙	○	○
Send change of address cards	△	△	⊙	
Bank acct.	⊙		△	
Newspaper			⊙	
Health club		⊙	△	
Church		⊙	△	
School	⊙		△	
Insurance		⊙	△	
Medical records	⊙		△	

assign family members to actions required to successfully move to a new location.

Matrix Data Analysis, Perceptual Map, and Glyph

Matrix data analysis is a sophisticated mathematical technique used to study the strengths of the interrelationships between two or more process or product characteristics. Figure

FIGURE 2–6
Example of Matrix Data Analysis

Purpose: Matrix data analysis is a sophisticated mathematical technique used to study the strengths of the interrelationships between two or more process or product characteristics.

Example:

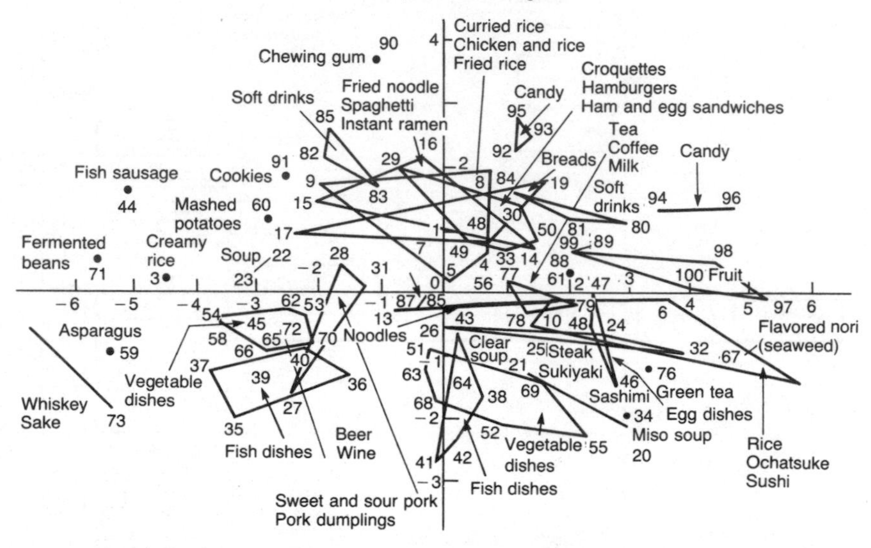

Source: Shigeru Mizuno, *Management for Quality Improvement: The 7 New QC Tools* (Cambridge, Mass.: Productivity Press, 1988), p. 206.

2–6 shows a matrix data analysis of food preferences in Japan. This book will not discuss this technique. Instead, Chapter 3 will discuss two related and simpler tools, a perceptual map and a glyph. Figure 2–7 shows a glyph used to choose a bank (see the "open a new bank account" card in the "settling in" category on the affinity diagram in Figure 2–2).

Process Decision Program Chart

The process decision program chart (PDPC) develops contingency plans. This tool is used with an unfamiliar process or product problem. Figure 2–8 shows contingency plans for the "get damage deposits back" category of the affinity diagram in Figure 2–2. The contingency plans are shown in the clouds

FIGURE 2–7
Example of Glyph

Problem Statement: Choosing the best bank.

Purpose: To evaluate several different alternatives based on three or more quality characteristics.

Example:

Criteria

A. Convenient location
B. Convenient hours
C. Price of services
D. Range of services
E. Quality of service (intangibles)

Financial institution

First National Bank
First Savings Bank
State Bank
Credit Union

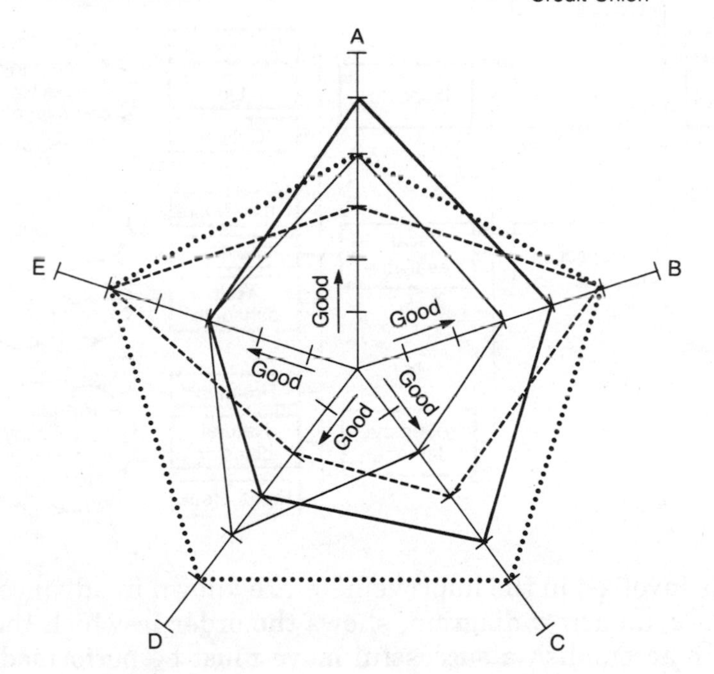

to the right of the systematic diagram branch for "getting damage deposit back."

Arrow Diagram

An arrow diagram is used to establish a time-sequenced action plan for implementing a process or product improvement when

FIGURE 2–8
Example of PDPC Analysis

Problem
Statement: What could affect getting the damage deposit back?

Purpose: The purpose of a PDPC analysis is to develop contingency plans for preventing or dealing with potential problems before they actually arise.

Example:

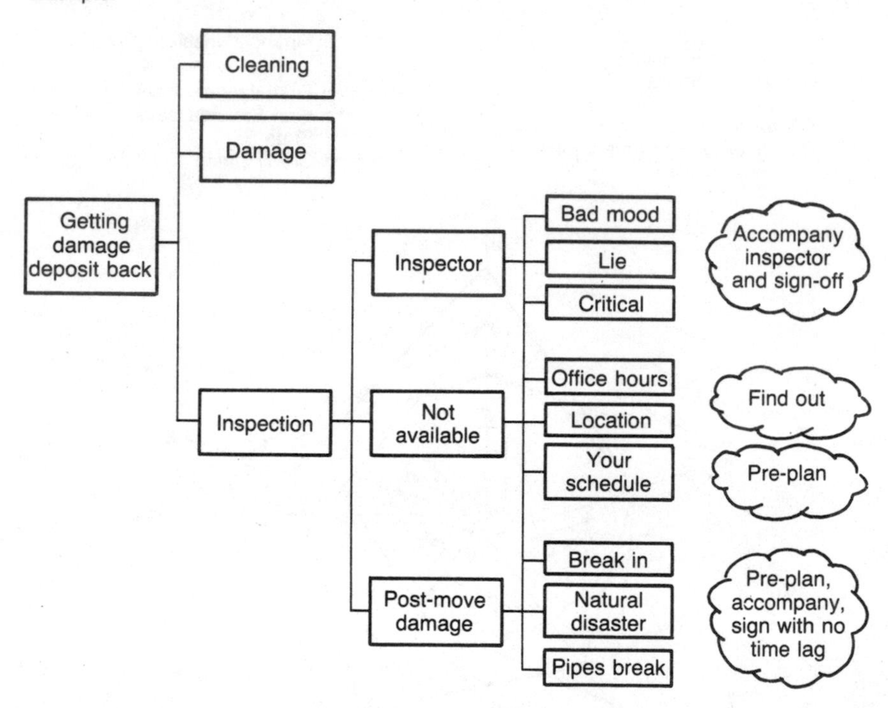

the steps involved in the improvement are known in advance. Figure 2–9, an arrow diagram, shows the order in which the actions to accomplish a successful move must be performed.

The Seven Basic Quality Control (QC) Tools

The second group of tools and methods, referred to as the seven basic QC tools, forms the backbone of any quality improvement efforts. The seven basic QC tools are extremely

FIGURE 2–9
Example of Arrow Diagram

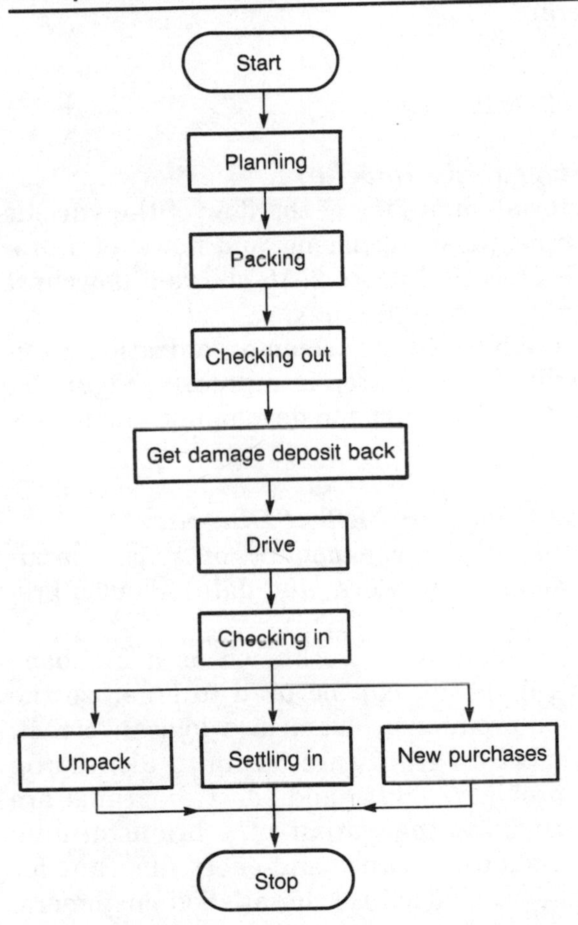

useful in studying the effectiveness of the countermeasures set into motion in the Do stage of the PDSA cycle. These tools are used by everyone in an organization, including salaried and hourly personnel, in their quality improvement efforts. They include:

1. Flowchart and integrated flowchart.
2. Brainstorming and cause-and-effect diagram.
3. Check sheet.

4. Pareto diagram and histogram.
5. Run chart and control chart.
6. Scatter diagram.
7. Stratification.

A brief description of each follows.

Flowchart and Integrated Flowchart

A flowchart is a pictorial summary of the flow of the various operations (for example, tasks, decisions, and flows) of a process. It documents a process. Figure 2–10 shows a flowchart of the steps in a quality of design study.

An integrated flowchart shows which organizational unit(s) is (are) responsible for each step in a process. Figure 2–11 shows an integrated flowchart for developing a software product.

Brainstorming and Cause-and-Effect Diagram

A team brainstorms to gather large amounts of creative input (including facts, opinions, guesswork, and data) about a process or product problem.

A cause-and-effect diagram, also known as a Fishbone diagram or Ishikawa diagram, can be used to organize the causes of a process or product problem in a logical format. Further, cause-and-effect diagrams are useful in identifying the root cause of a problem. Cause-and-effect diagrams are frequently used to organize the output of a brainstorming session. Figure 2–12 shows a cause-and-effect diagram for problems with shipments that cause dissatisfied customers.

Check Sheet

A check sheet is used to collect data about a product or process in an organized manner so the data can be analyzed with a statistical tool; for example, a Pareto diagram, histogram, run chart, or control chart. Figure 2–13 shows three types of check sheets.

Pareto Diagram and Histogram

A Pareto diagram separates the "significant few" product or process problems from the "trivial many" product or process

FIGURE 2–10
Example of Flowchart

Quality-of-design study

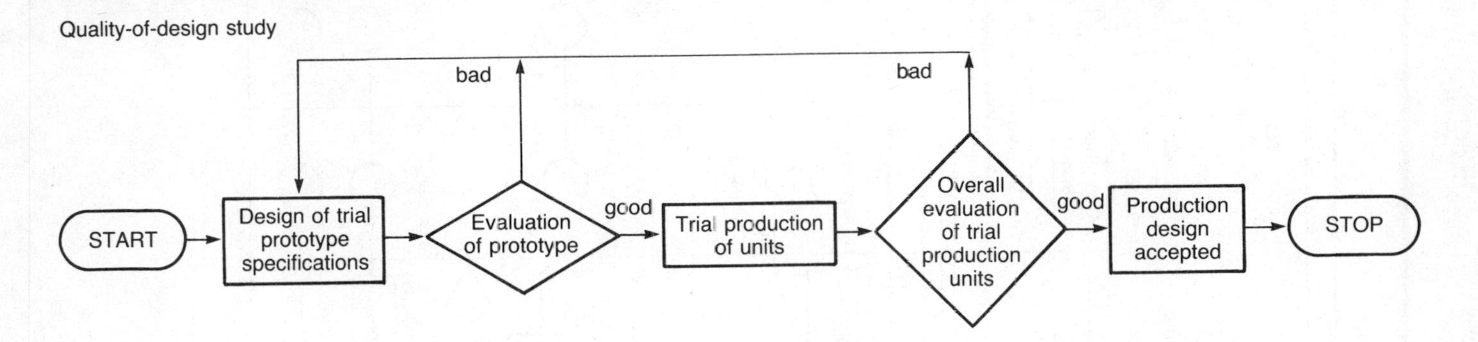

Source: H. Gitlow, S. Gitlow, A. Oppenheim, and R. Oppenheim, *Tools and Methods for the Improvement of Quality* (Homewood, Ill.: Richard D. Irwin, Inc., 1989), p. 43

FIGURE 2–11
Example of Integrated Flowchart

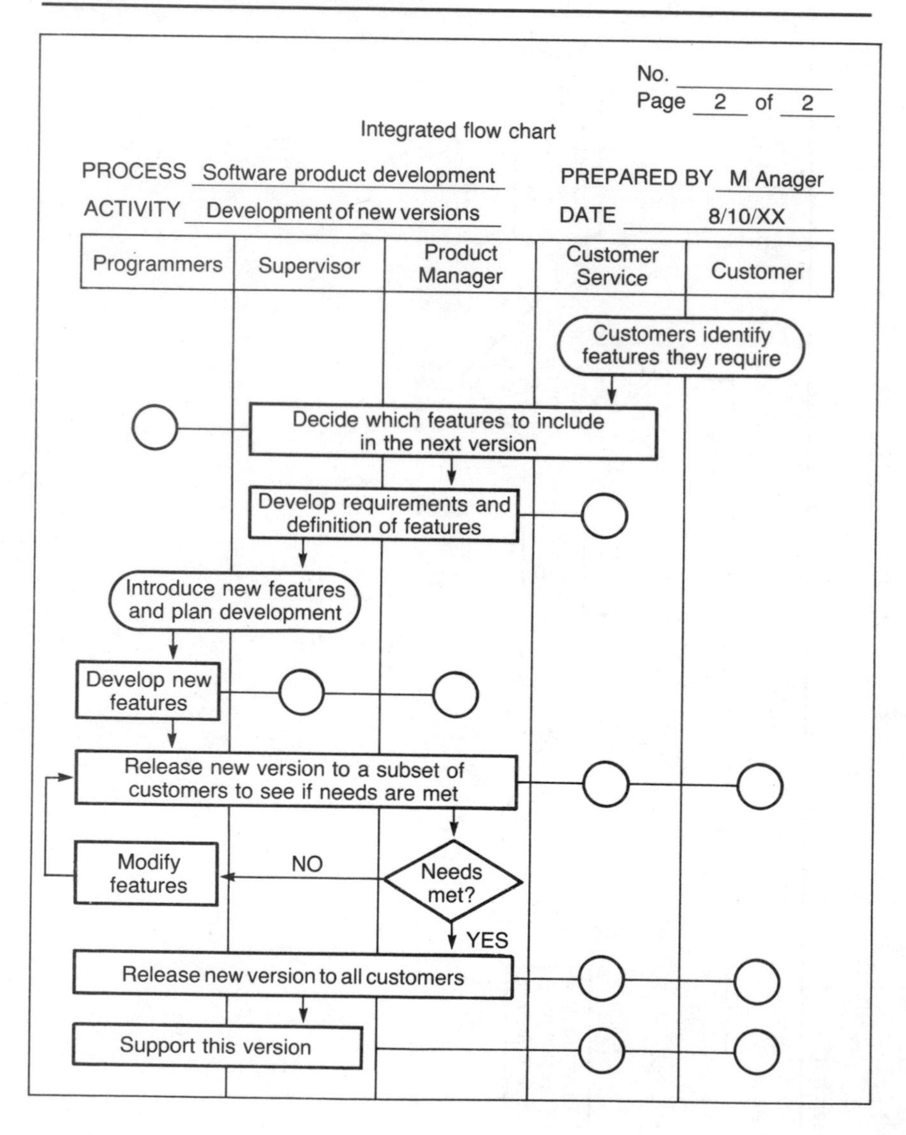

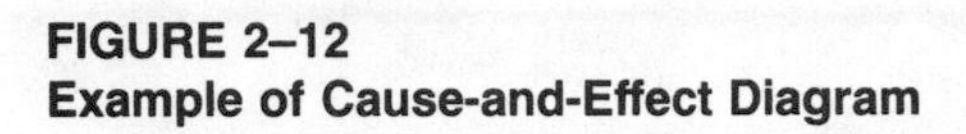

FIGURE 2–12
Example of Cause-and-Effect Diagram

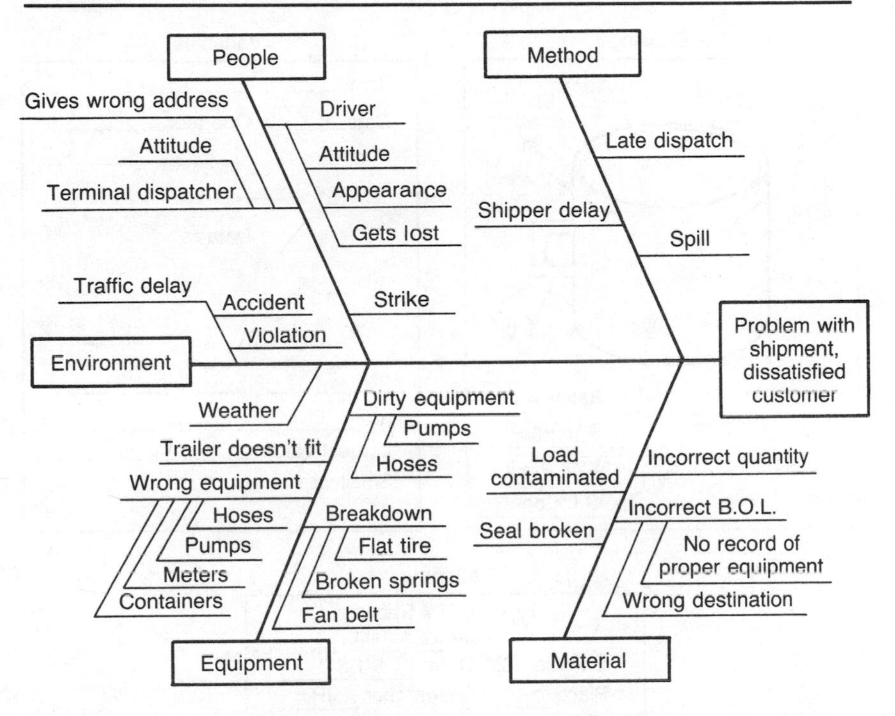

problems. Hence, a Pareto diagram can be used to establish priorities in respect to process or product problems. Figure 2–14 shows a Pareto diagram of the types of defects in an assembly operation.

A histogram constructs a pictorial representation of a frequency distribution for a measurable process or product characteristic. Figure 2–15 shows a histogram of product weights from a production line.

Run Chart and Control Chart

A run chart is usually a time-sequenced plot of a quality characteristic. Figure 2–16 shows a run chart of the number of bad checks per day for 21 days.

A control chart can be used to distinguish special causes of variation from system causes of variation. Consequently,

FIGURE 2–13
Examples of Check Sheets

A Drawing

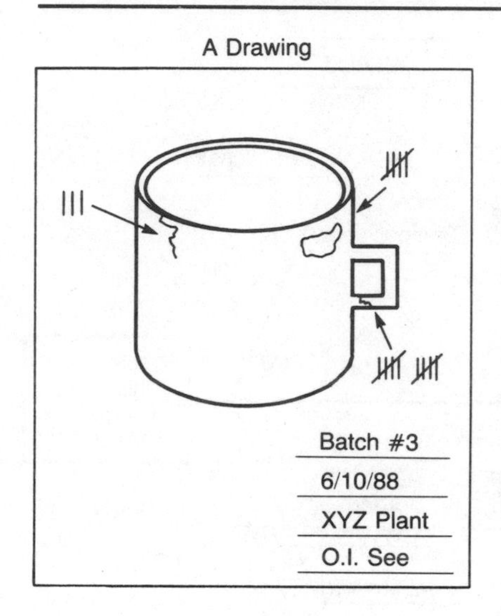

Variables

Item ______
Date ______ Operator ______
Plant ______
Purpose ______

Data

n = ______
Largest value ______
Smallest value ______

Attribute

Types of TV Shows
Watched by Adults
Sample 20 Date 8/1-8/2
Place ______ Researcher JP

Show Type	Tally	Total
Drama	~~IIII~~ ~~IIII~~ II	12
Special	~~IIII~~	5
Comedy	~~IIII~~ II	7
Sports	~~IIII~~ ~~IIII~~ ~~IIII~~	15
Game Show	~~IIII~~ III	8
Total Shows Watched		47

a control chart can help management decide how to act in a given situation, that is, a problem-solving action to resolve a special cause of variation, or a system-improvement action to eliminate a system cause of variation. Figure 2–17 shows three examples of control charts. Cases one and three are out of control, while case two is in control.

FIGURE 2–14
Example of Pareto Diagram

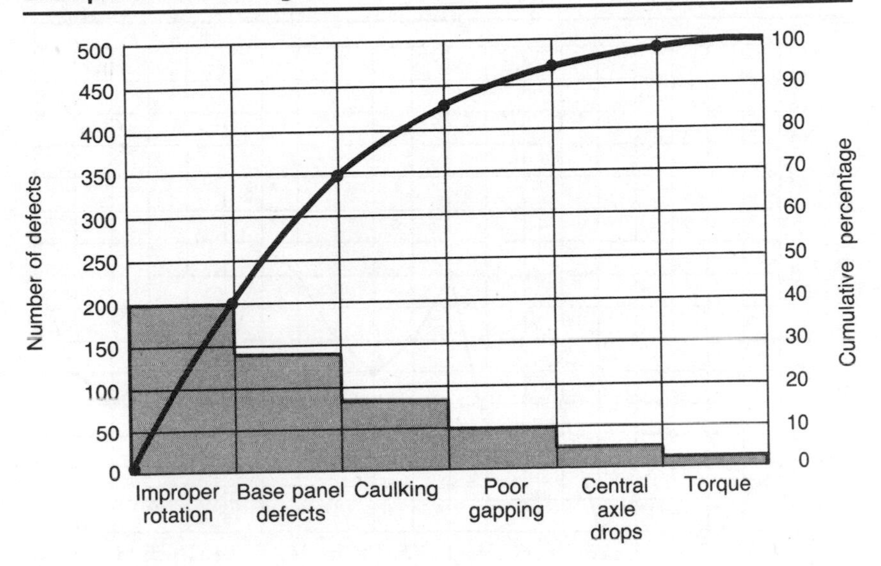

FIGURE 2–15
Example of Histogram

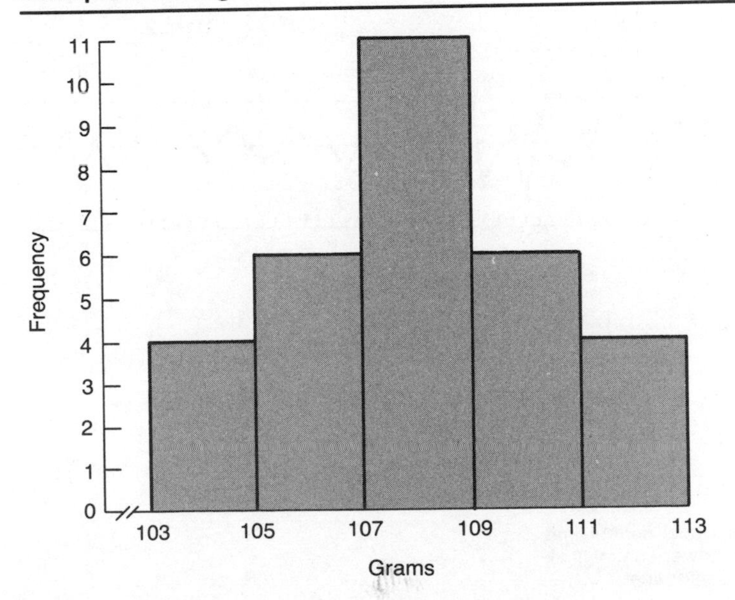

FIGURE 2–16
Example of Run Chart

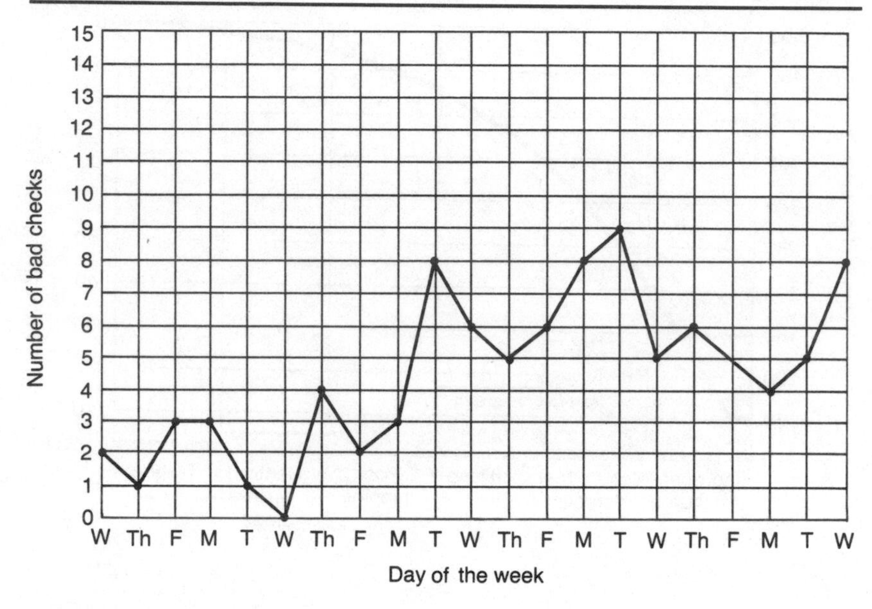

FIGURE 2–17
Examples of Control Charts

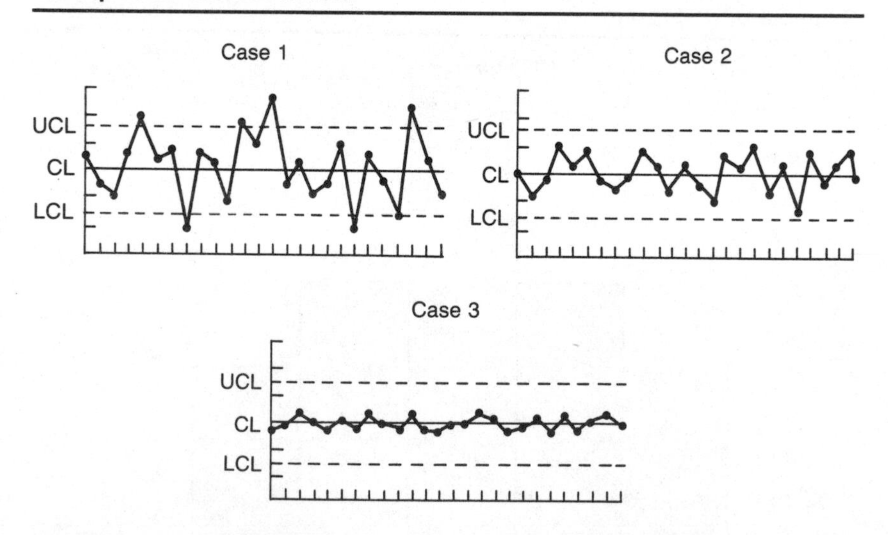

UCL = Upper control limit
LCL = Lower control limit
CL = Center line

Scatter Diagram

A scatter diagram graphically depicts the strength and direction of the relationship between two process or product characteristics. Figure 2–18 shows a scatter diagram of the relationship between height and weight for adults.

Stratification

Stratification systematically breaks down a set of data about a process or product characteristic into smaller subgroups so it is possible to determine the root cause of the process or product problems. Figure 2–19 shows an example of stratification.

FIGURE 2–18
Example of Scatter Diagram

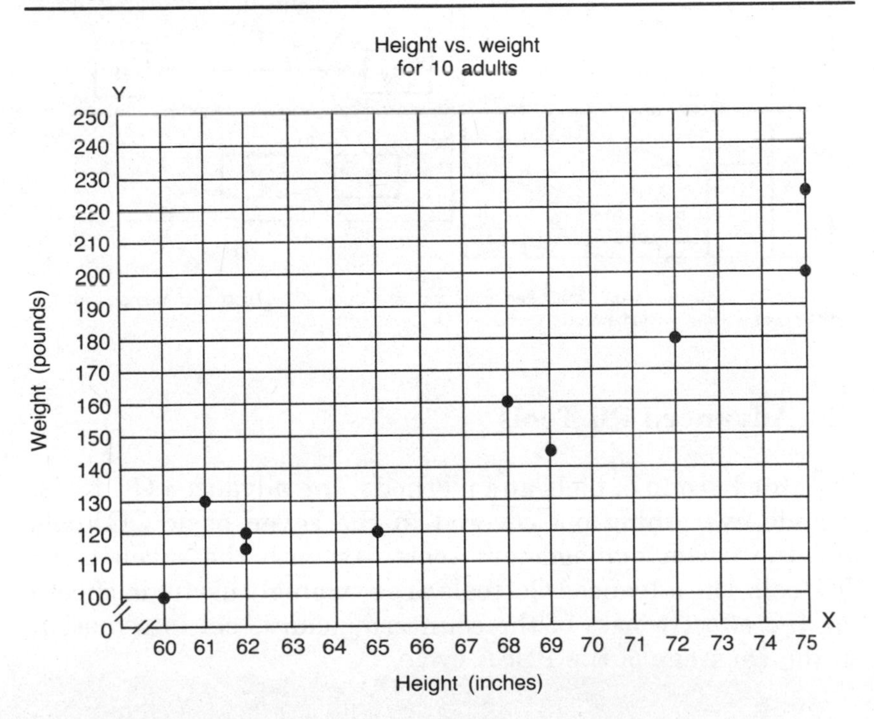

FIGURE 2–19
Example of Stratification

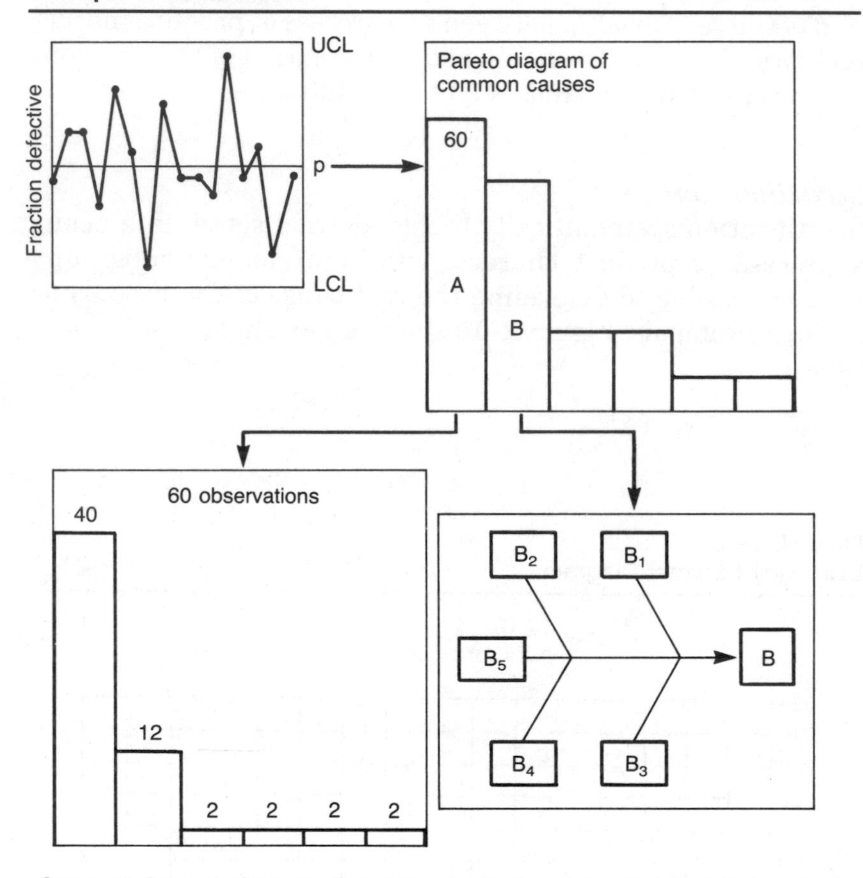

Source: H. Gitlow, S. Gitlow, A. Oppenheim, and R. Oppenheim, *Tools and Methods for the Improvement of Quality* (Homewood, Ill.: Richard D. Irwin, Inc.), p. 406.

The Advanced QC Tools

The third group of tools and methods, the advanced QC tools, include everything not covered in the seven basic QC tools and the seven management tools. As with the seven basic QC tools, the advanced QC tools are extremely useful in checking the effectiveness of the countermeasures set into motion in the Do stage of the PDSA cycle.

The advanced QC tools include design of experiments, Taguchi experiments, regression analysis, multivariate analysis (for example, factor analysis, discriminant analysis, canonical correlation, cluster analysis), and sampling plans.

Overview

The above tools and methods provide a powerful set of diagnostic devices that can be used in the PDSA cycle to decrease the difference between customer needs and process performance. Figure 2–20 shows some of the possible uses of the seven management tools, the seven basic QC tools, and the advanced QC tools with respect to the stages of the PDSA cycle.

FIGURE 2–20
Tools and Methods of the PDSA Cycle

PDSA Cycle Stages	*7 M Tools*	*7 Basic QC Tools*	*Advanced Tools*
Plan	Affinity	Flowchart	
	Interrelationship diagraph		
	Systematic	Brainstorming & Cause-and-effect	Taguchi
	Matrix		Multivariate
	Matrix data		
	PDPC		
	Arrow		
Do			
Study		Check sheet	Multivariate
		Pareto	Sampling plans
		Histograms	Design of experiments
		Control charts	Regression
		Scatter	
		Stratification	
Act			

CONSENSUS DECISION-MAKING AND THE SEVEN MANAGEMENT TOOLS[4]

Overview

If a team is going to use the seven management tools to develop a plan for decreasing the difference between customer needs and process performance, the team must reach consensus with respect to the plan. Many of the seven management tools require consensus decision-making as an integral part of their use by a team.

In consensus decision-making, the members of a team reach decisions that reflect the thinking of all team members; decisions are acceptable to all team members and unacceptable to no team member. Consensus decision-making is not a unanimous vote, because a unanimous vote may not reflect each team member's first decision priority. It is also not a majority vote because only the majority's priorities are reflected in the final decision. Neither is it a process that creates total satisfaction for all members of a team.

Implications of Consensus Decision-Making

Consensus decision-making requires that: (1) all team members have a chance to voice their point of view with respect to the problem discussed, (2) the team must find a solution to the problem that meets the needs of all team members and is acceptable to all team members, (3) enough time is allocated to discussion of the problem so team members have a chance to buy in to a decision, (4) team members commit to follow through with the decision in a consistent manner outside of the meeting, (5) all data relevant to the problem have been made available to all team members, (6) voting is not done in an attempt to resolve the problem, and (7) the problem is important enough to require the support of all team members. A team that does not consider the seven issues stated above will not be able to use consensus decision-making to solve a problem.

Methods for Reaching a Decision

A team can use three methods to reach a decision about a problem: multivoting, nominal group technique, and negotiation.

Multivoting

In multivoting, a team repeatedly votes on a set of issues, ideas, proposals, or actions. After each vote, the issue, idea, proposal, or action with the least votes is dropped from the plan. This process continues until one issue, idea, proposal, or action remains.

Nominal Group Technique

Nominal group technique (NGT) is much like multivoting, but in NGT, team members individually assign point values to each issue, idea, proposal, or action. After each vote, the issue, idea, proposal, or action with the least votes is dropped from the plan. This process continues until one issue, idea, proposal, or action remains.

Negotiation

Negotiation occurs when team members freely discuss their issues, ideas, proposals, or actions with respect to a plan until they are satisfied with the plan. Unlike multivoting and NGT, negotiation does not have an artificial endpoint triggered by a vote; negotiation continues until all team members can buy in to a plan. Consequently, negotiation can be slow and frustrating. But, in the end, negotiation will sustain the greatest degree of team member acceptance of a plan. Negotiation is consensus decision-making.

Decision-Making and the Seven Management Tools

Because of the need for some decision-making process when working with the seven management tools, a team will find itself using either multivoting, NGT, or negotiation. Which method to use must be determined in light of a team's ability to reach a consensus. If a team can easily reach a consensus, then negotiation may be preferred. However, if a team does not have a great facility to reach a consensus, then either multivoting or NGT is preferred.

Quality improvement plans developed using the seven management tools will work best if they are prepared in an environment that encourages consensus decision-making, allowing team members to buy in to the plan.

CHAPTER SUMMARY

This chapter presents a detailed description of the PDSA cycle, which is used to decrease the difference between customer needs and process performance. The PDSA cycle comprises four basic stages: (1) **P**lan stage, (2) **D**o stage, (3) **S**tudy stage, and (4) **A**ct stage. A plan is developed (Plan), the plan is tested on a small scale or trial basis (Do), the effects of the trial plan are monitored (Study), and appropriate process improvements are made (Act). These improvement actions, called *countermeasures,* can lead to a new or revised plan or process modifications, and so the PDSA cycle continuously decreases the difference between customer needs and process performance.

Next, the chapter presents an overview of the tools and methods of the PDSA cycle. The tools and methods fall into three categories: the seven management tools, the seven basic QC tools, and the advanced QC tools. The seven management tools are: (1) affinity diagrams, (2) interrelationship diagraphs, (3) systematic diagrams, (4) matrix diagrams, (5) matrix data analysis, (6) PDPC analysis, and (7) arrow diagrams. The seven basic QC tools are: (1) flowchart and integrated flowchart, (2) brainstorming and cause-and-effect diagram, (3) check sheet, (4) pareto diagram and histogram, (5) run chart and control chart, (6) scatter diagram, and (7) stratification. The advanced QC tools include design of experiments, Taguchi experiments, regression analysis, multivariate analysis (for example, factor analysis, discriminant analysis, canonical correlation, cluster analysis), and sampling plans.

Finally, the chapter discusses three methods for decision-making: nominal group technique, multivoting, and negotiation. Negotiation is shown to be the only decision-making form in which a team can reach a consensus. Finally, the importance of consensus decision-making to proper use of the seven management tools is explained.

ENDNOTES

1. William Scherkenbach, *The Deming Route to Quality and Productivity: Road Maps and Road Blocks* (Washington, D.C.: Cee-Press Books, 1986), pp. 35–40.
2. Dr. W. E. Deming objects to the use of the word *check* when describing this stage of the PDSA cycle because "to check" means to hold back.
3. Kaoru Ishikawa, *What Is Total Quality Control? The Japanese Way* (Englewood Cliffs, N.J.: Prentice-Hall, 1985), pp. 59–71.
4. The material in this section is heavily drawn from Peter Scholtes et al., *The TEAM Handbook: How to Use Teams to Improve Quality* (Madison, Wis.: Joiner Associates, Inc., 1988).

CHAPTER 3

PLANNING FOR QUALITY WITH THE SEVEN MANAGEMENT TOOLS

INTRODUCTION

As stated in Chapter 2, the seven management tools are extremely valuable in formulating the plan to be used in the PDSA cycle to decrease the difference between customer needs and process performance. Planning using the seven management tools utilizes a three-phase process.

The first phase identifies product or process problem(s) whose resolution will decrease the difference between customer needs and process performance. The affinity diagram and the interrelationship diagraph are the major tools of phase one. A team can use the affinity diagram to generate, organize, and consolidate a large amount of verbal information about a product or process problem into natural clusters that bring out the latent structure of the problem under study. The interrelationship diagraph can identify the logical and sequential relationships between the product or process problem under study and related ideas.

The second planning phase determines the action(s) needed to resolve the product or process problem(s) discovered in phase one. The systematic diagram, matrix diagram, glyph, and perceptual map are the major tools of phase two. A team can use the systematic diagram to determine the root cause of a problem or to generate the actions required to solve a problem. The matrix diagram can help a team to relate the product or process problem with other issues, such as assigning people to the actions required to resolve the problem. A team can use the glyph and the perceptual map to probe deeply into the multifaceted relationships that exist between quality, cost, scheduling, quantity, and delivery with respect to product and process problems.

The third phase focuses on developing the time sequencing and contingency plans for the action(s) developed in phase two. PDPC analysis and the arrow diagram are the major tools of phase three. A team can use PDPC analysis to develop contingency plans for the actions developed in phase two. The arrow diagram can help develop the sequencing and timing for the entire plan. The output from phases one, two, and three form a plan for decreasing the difference between customer needs and process performance. The likelihood of the planning process yielding a success story increases with team consensus in the planning process.

Figure 3–1 provides an overview of how each of the seven management tools is related to the others and to the phases of the planning process. Figure 3–2 shows a sequence for using the seven management tools that promotes planning to solve a product or process problem. The affinity diagram ascertains the latent issues underlying a problem. The interrelationship diagraph determines the cause-and-effect relationships between the underlying issues discerned in the affinity diagram. The systematic diagram organizes the cause-and-effect relationships determined by the interrelationship diagraph and identifies the actions required to resolve the problem under study. The matrix diagram balances workloads and assigns people to positions of responsibility for executing the actions determined in the systematic diagram. The glyph and perceptual map further study a problem. PDPC analysis develops contingency plans to increase the likelihood of success when implementing the action items developed in the systematic diagram. Finally, the arrow diagram develops the sequencing and time-based scheduling required to carry out the plan.

FIGURE 3–1
Overview of the Seven Management Tools in Planning

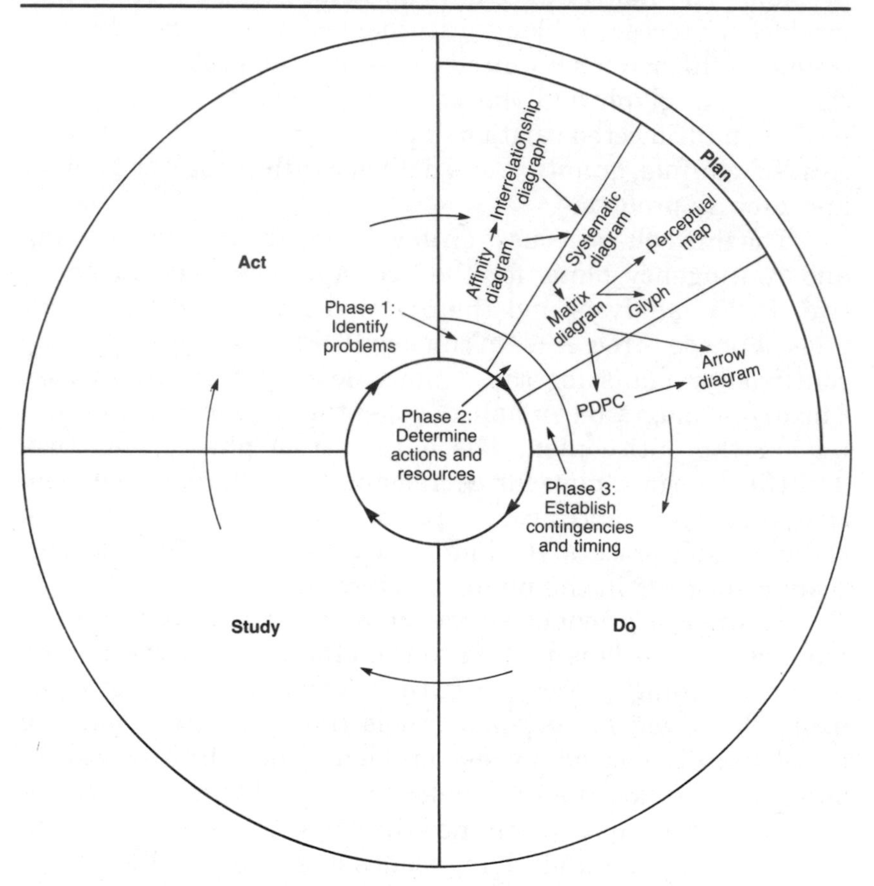

PHASE ONE: IDENTIFYING PRODUCT OR PROCESS PROBLEMS WHOSE RESOLUTION WILL DECREASE THE DIFFERENCE BETWEEN CUSTOMER NEEDS AND PROCESS PERFORMANCE

Introduction

The first step in establishing a plan that will resolve a product or process problem is collecting and organizing information about the problem. This information can include numeric data, verbal data, ideas, facts, guesses, and opinions. Organizing this information will help move from creative amorphous thoughts to logical relationships (see affinity diagram) and from general and nonspecific product or process problems to logical relationships (see interrelationship diagraph). The affinity diagram and interrelationship diagraph can help determine logical relationships between product or process problems, which are important in formulating a product or process improvement plan.

Affinity Diagram

A group (or team) can use the affinity diagram to generate, organize, and consolidate an extensive and unorganized amount of verbal information concerning a product or process problem. The verbal information usually consists of facts, opinions, intuition, and experience. The affinity diagram helps organize this information into natural clusters that bring out the latent structure of the problem under study. It is a creative rather than logical process.

Current problems may not respond to established thinking patterns. An affinity diagram can help a group break free from established thinking. Affinity diagrams promote creative, rather than standard, solutions to problems.

Affinity diagrams are particularly useful if the problem under study:

1. Is complex and difficult to get a handle on.
2. Requires a lot of time to solve.
3. Has not responded to traditional (well-established) solutions.
4. Requires the involvement of group members to be solved.

Affinity diagrams are not useful if the problem is simple or requires an immediate solution.

Construction

Constructing an affinity diagram begins with identifying a problem and appropriate team members. Team composition will depend on the problem being studied. The four- or five-

FIGURE 3–2
Generic Example of Planning with the Seven Management Tools

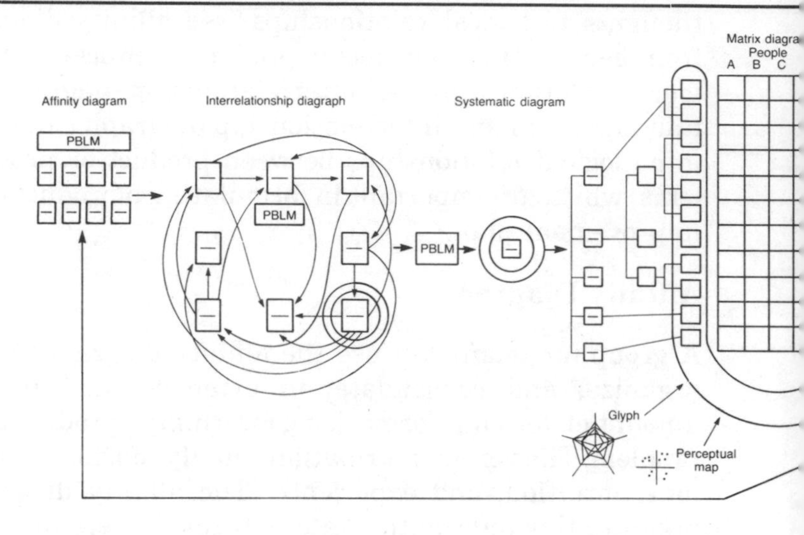

member team should include a variety of people, not all of whom should be technical experts about the product or process problem. For example, a team meeting to study problems encountered in purchasing component parts could consist of a purchasing agent, an engineer, a maintenance person, the operator who uses the component part, and his or her supervisor.

A team should take the following steps to construct an affinity diagram:

1. Select a team member to serve as the group's facilitator.

2. Have the group's facilitator write a question about a product or process problem on a flip chart and allow the group members to think about it creatively.

3. Encourage team members to individually think about and then discuss as a group the product or process problem; this may involve the use of multivoting, NGT, or negotiation. The discussion should last between 30 and 45 minutes. The facilitator should write down the group members' verbal information on small cards or on a flip chart (to be transferred to small cards later) exactly as it is stated so its essence is

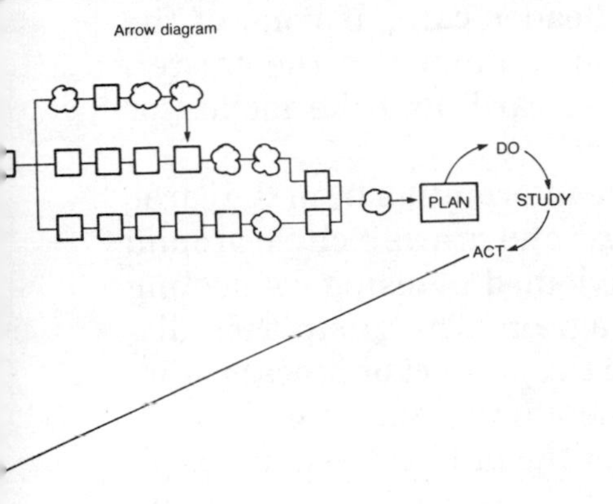

preserved. Another alternative is to have each person record his or her own ideas on 3×5 cards or Post-it™ Notes.[1]

4. Once the team decides that the discussion has ended and all the verbal information has been written down by the group's facilitator, he or she should spread all the cards on a large working surface in no particular order.

5. All group members should simultaneously move the cards into clusters so the cards in a cluster seem to be related. One team member may move a card to one cluster, and another team member may move the card back to its former cluster; this may go on for a time, but the card will eventually find a home cluster.

Group members continue to move the cards until meaningful clusters form. Clustering is finished once group members begin to speak to each other. If clustering continues for too long, too few piles may remain, thereby hiding the latent structure of the problem. Cards that do not fit into any cluster should be placed in a miscellaneous cluster. This step is most effective if performed without talking.

6. After the group agrees the clusters are complete (usually 7 to 10 clusters emerge), the group selects a card from each cluster that sums up the information in that cluster; that card becomes the cluster's header card. If none of the cards summarizes the information contained in the cluster, then the group agrees on a header card, and the facilitator prepares it.

7. The facilitator transfers the information from the cards onto a flip chart, or "butcher paper," and draws a circle around each cluster. Related clusters are joined by using connecting lines; this is called an affinity diagram. The group then discusses the cluster's relationship to the product or process problem and makes any changes to the affinity diagram.

8. The underlying structure of the problem, usually typified by the names of the header cards, is used to understand the product or process problem under investigation.

Figure 3–3 shows an integrated flowchart of how to construct an affinity diagram.

Example

A team of employees in a company addressed the question: "What are the problems in achieving a total quality transformation?" The team recorded its ideas on cards. When they placed the cards on a table, all team members took several turns moving the cards. When everyone agreed on the clusters, they found that seven clusters had emerged; one cluster had a single card. Figure 3–4 shows the resulting affinity diagram.

In Figure 3–4, the team's view of the problems in achieving a total quality transformation are given by the header cards:

1. Departmental barriers.
2. Fear.
3. Organizational practices.
4. Working with suppliers.
5. Training.
6. Empowerment.
7. Individual buy-in.

A detailed study of the above seven categories will help the group understand the problems in achieving a total quality transformation.

FIGURE 3–3
Integrated Flowchart of How to Construct an Affinity Diagram

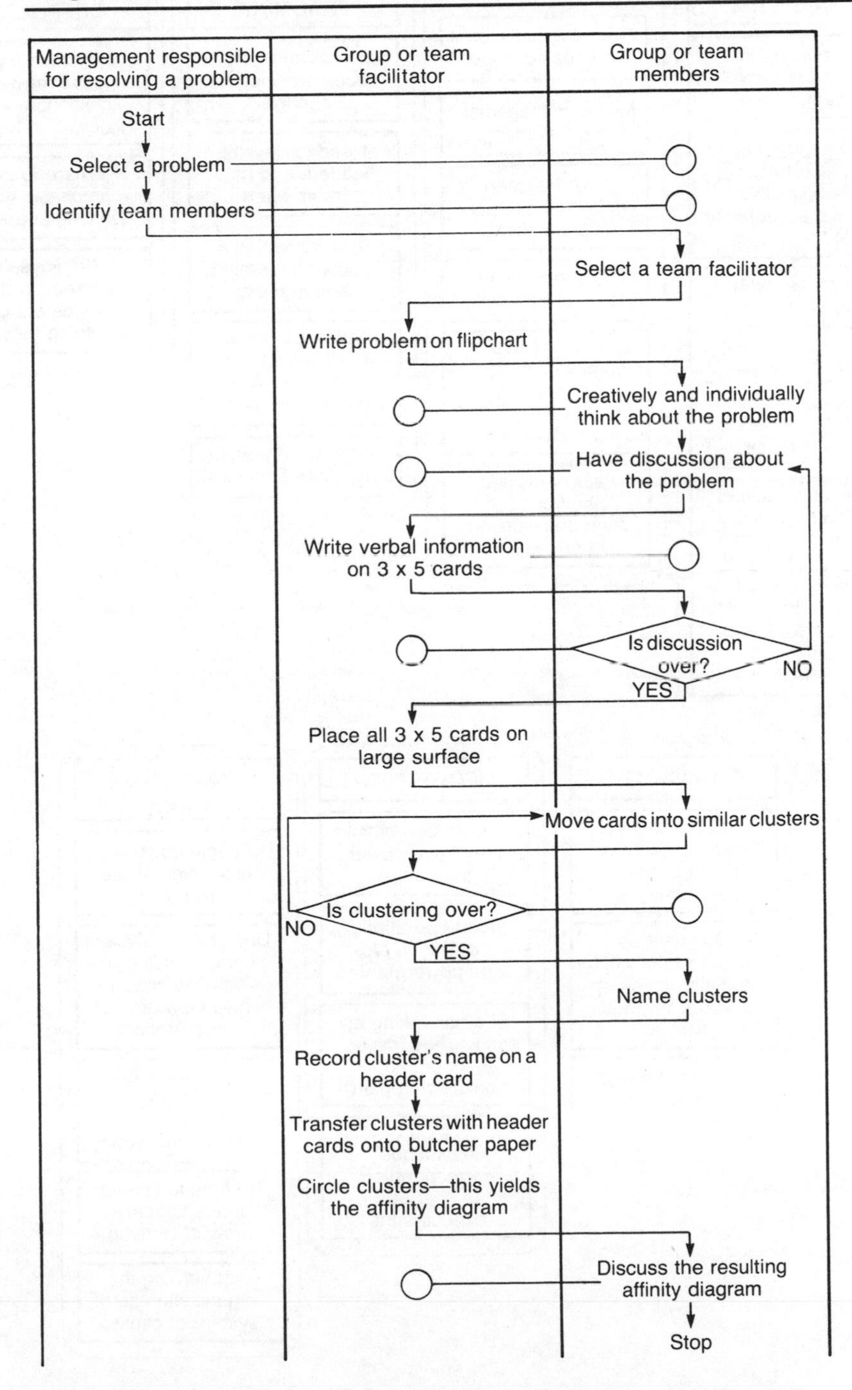

FIGURE 3–4
Affinity Diagram—What Are the Problems in Achieving a Total Quality Transformation?

DEPARTMENTAL BARRIERS	FEAR	ORGANIZATIONAL PRACTICES	WORKING WITH SUPPLIERS
People on the floor can't make suggestions	Fear of termination if we don't change	Do managers have competencies to change?	Difficult to move upstream when philosophy not followed in-house
Organizational "labeling" of people limits others' acceptance of their views	Middle management afraid of change	Need to develop leaders and help them learn	Where to put emphasis with Deming suppliers
Encouraging independence keeps people from collaborating	Fear between middle and upper management	Reward systems, bonuses, profit sharing, etc.	Employee's perception that customers get everything they want
Sub-optimization of departments, no overall plan	There are barriers to applying ideas	Difficult to move from fire-fighting mode to problem prevention mode	
Negative view of teams' ability to make decisions	Do we have commitment from management, or mere compliance?	We reward people who fight fires well	
Established culture focuses on results, distorts internal customer/supplier relationships	Fear of moving out of comfort zone and working in new ways		

TRAINING	EMPOWERMENT	INDIVIDUAL BUY-IN
Training to meet arbitrary goals vs. training to change performance	People don't think they have power to change	People don't see grounding of the 14 points
Don't set up structure to facilitate transformation in conjunction with training	Need operational definition of empowerment	Don't have sufficient understanding or belief to create new view of the organization
Training process is too long	See risk-taking as "minimizing losses" as opposed to "maximizing gain"	Use tools to understand variation and Deming philosophy
	No change of role definitions corresponding to changed expectations	No time to change management's view of Deming
		Not viewing the organization as a "system of causes"

Workshop on the Affinity Diagram

Teams preparing to construct an affinity diagram will need the following supplies:

1. Five packages of 3 × 5 cards or five packages of 3 × 4 Post-it™ Notes.
2. One flip chart.
3. One roll of butcher paper.
4. One scissor to cut the butcher paper.
5. Pens (one per participant).
6. Pads (one per participant).

Interrelationship Diagraph (Diagram/Graph)

The interrelationship diagraph (ID) permits a team to identify the logical and sequential connections between a product or process problem and related ideas. The team generates many ideas related to the problem. The group then identifies patterns between the problem and the generated ideas. The ID portrays the logical and sequential relationships between the product or process problem and the generated ideas.

The cards generated from an affinity diagram are frequently the starting point for an ID. Three common methods for using affinity diagram cards as input into an interrelationship diagraph are:

1. Use only the header cards from the affinity diagram. This method focuses the diagraph on the sequential and logical relationships between the ideas that form the latent structure of the problem.
2. Use the cards under one header card. This method focuses the diagraph on the sequential and logical relationships between the ideas that comprise one of the basic building blocks (latent structure) of the problem.
3. Use all the cards from the affinity diagram. This method focuses the diagraph on all aspects of the problem, but this method can yield a cumbersome ID.

It is always possible to brainstorm for ideas to use in an interrelationship diagraph.

Interrelationship diagraphs are particularly useful if the problem under study:

1. Has complex cause-and-effect relationships or complex objective-to-means (method to go from A to B) relationships with related ideas.
2. Requires an understanding of its interrelationship of a problem with new ideas and concepts (this eliminates preconceived views for solution of the problem).
3. Requires a thorough understanding of its logical and sequential relationships with related ideas.
4. Is believed to be a symptom and not a root problem.
5. Requires a lot of time to solve.
6. Requires the involvement of several individuals, possibly in several departments, to be solved (buy-in by consensus).

Interrelationship diagraphs are not useful if the problem is simple or requires an immediate solution.

Construction

A team should take the following steps to construct an interrelationship diagraph.

1. Management identifies a product or process problem to study. The problem statement should include at least one noun and one verb. This product or process problem may come from an affinity diagram or some other source.

2. Management identifies a team appropriate for solving the problem. The composition of the team will depend on the product or process problem being studied. The team should include a variety of people, not all of whom should be technical experts about the product or process problem under study. Team size is ideally four or five participants.

3. Team members should select a facilitator who will record the problem on a card or flip chart.

4. The problem statement can be placed in the middle of the work space (the centralized pattern) or at the right or left of the work space (the unidirectional pattern). The centralized pattern is utilized when many ideas are closely connected to the problem statement. The unidirectional pattern is used when fewer ideas are closely related to the problem statement.

5. Draw a double-lined circle (also known as double hatching) around the statement of the problem.

6a. If the problem statement was drawn from an affinity diagram, team members should arrange all the cards in the affinity diagram so the cards containing the ideas most closely related to the problem statement are close to the card containing the problem statement. Conversely, team members should move the cards least related to the problem farther away from the problem card. If a card contains an idea that is a link between two or more other idea cards, team members should place this card between the related cards. Team members should shift the position of the cards containing the ideas until the group achieves consensus on the positioning of the idea cards with respect to the problem card. The team may want to brainstorm for more ideas to fill in any gaps about the problem.

Two possible variants of step 6a are: (1) to use only the problem statement and header cards from an affinity diagram to make an interrelationship diagraph, or (2) to use only one of the header cards as a problem statement and its supporting idea cards from an affinity diagram to make an interrelationship diagraph. Additional brainstorming can be done to generate more idea cards with both variants of step 6a.

6b. If the problem statement was derived from a source other than an affinity diagram, the team will need to brainstorm for ideas related to the statement. The facilitator should write the ideas on individual cards. (Because of team members' need to shift ideas around until they reach consensus, putting the ideas directly on the flip chart is not recommended.) Again, team members should arrange all the cards so the cards containing the ideas most closely related to the problem statement are close to the card containing the problem statement and those least related to the problem are farther away. If a card contains an idea that is a link between two or more other idea cards, team members should place this card between the related idea cards. Team members should shift the position of the cards until the group achieves consensus on the positioning of the idea cards. The team may want to brainstorm more to fill in any gaps about ideas relating to the problem.

7. Draw a line connecting pairs of related idea cards. Consider the problem statement as just another idea card for this part of the analysis. An arrowhead (known as a causal arrow) at the end of a line will indicate the direction of the cause-and-effect relationship characterized by the line. The idea card with the arrowhead pointing to it is the effect, while the idea card with the arrow pointing away from it is the cause. Use only one-way arrows. The team must decide which direction is the stronger cause-and-effect direction.

8. For each card, count the number of arrows moving away and moving into the card. Place both counts on the top of the card as follows: (number away, number into).

9. Identify the key cause factor by determining which card has the most arrows moving away from it. Enclose the key cause factor in a double-hatched box.

10. Identify the key effect factor by determining which card has the most arrows moving into it.

11. Identify the sequence of intermediate cause factors between the key cause factor, the key effect factor, and the problem statement.

12. Create a legible copy of the interrelationship diagraph and circulate copies of it to the team members. Repeat this step several times to achieve consensus on the diagraph.

13. Use the diagraph as an aid in solving the problem under study.

Three types of meetings are needed to construct an interrelationship diagraph until group members feel comfortable with it. Type one meetings determine the problem, probe the possible causes of the problem, and study the interrelationships between the problem and its possible causes. Every effort should be made to keep all written comments close to their original form. Type one meetings should be held for two hours once or twice a week.

Type two meetings focus attention on the possible causes of the problem to determine where data are required to study their effect on the problem, where data are available to study their effect on the problem, and where action should be taken, action must be taken, and action should not be taken. Consensus among team members is required in classifying the possible causes as stated above. Type two meetings should be held for two hours once or twice a week until group members feel comfortable with their classifications of causes.

Type three meetings review the results of actions taken in type two meetings and revise the diagraph due to current conditions. Type three meetings should be held for two hours once or twice a week.

An integrated flowchart of how to construct an interrelationship diagraph is shown in Figure 3–5.

Example

The team investigating "What are the problems in achieving a total quality transformation?" wanted a better understanding of the interrelationships underlying the latent structure determined in the affinity diagram in Figure 3–4. To this end, an interrelationship diagraph was constructed using the header cards from the affinity diagram in Figure 3–4. The resulting interrelationship diagraph appears in Figure 3–6. Figure 3–6 shows that "training" and "organizational practices" are two root causes that must be addressed in achieving a total quality transformation.

Workshop on the Interrelationship Diagraph

A team preparing to construct an interrelationship diagraph will need the following supplies.

1. Five packages of 3 × 5 cards or five packages of 3 × 4 Post-it™ Notes.
2. One flip chart.
3. One roll of butcher paper.
4. One scissor to cut the butcher paper.
5. Pens (one per participant).
6. Pads (one per participant).

Summary

The output from phase one should be the isolation of problems whose resolution will decrease the difference between customer needs and process performance.

FIGURE 3–5
Integrated Flowchart of How to Construct an Interrelationship Diagraph

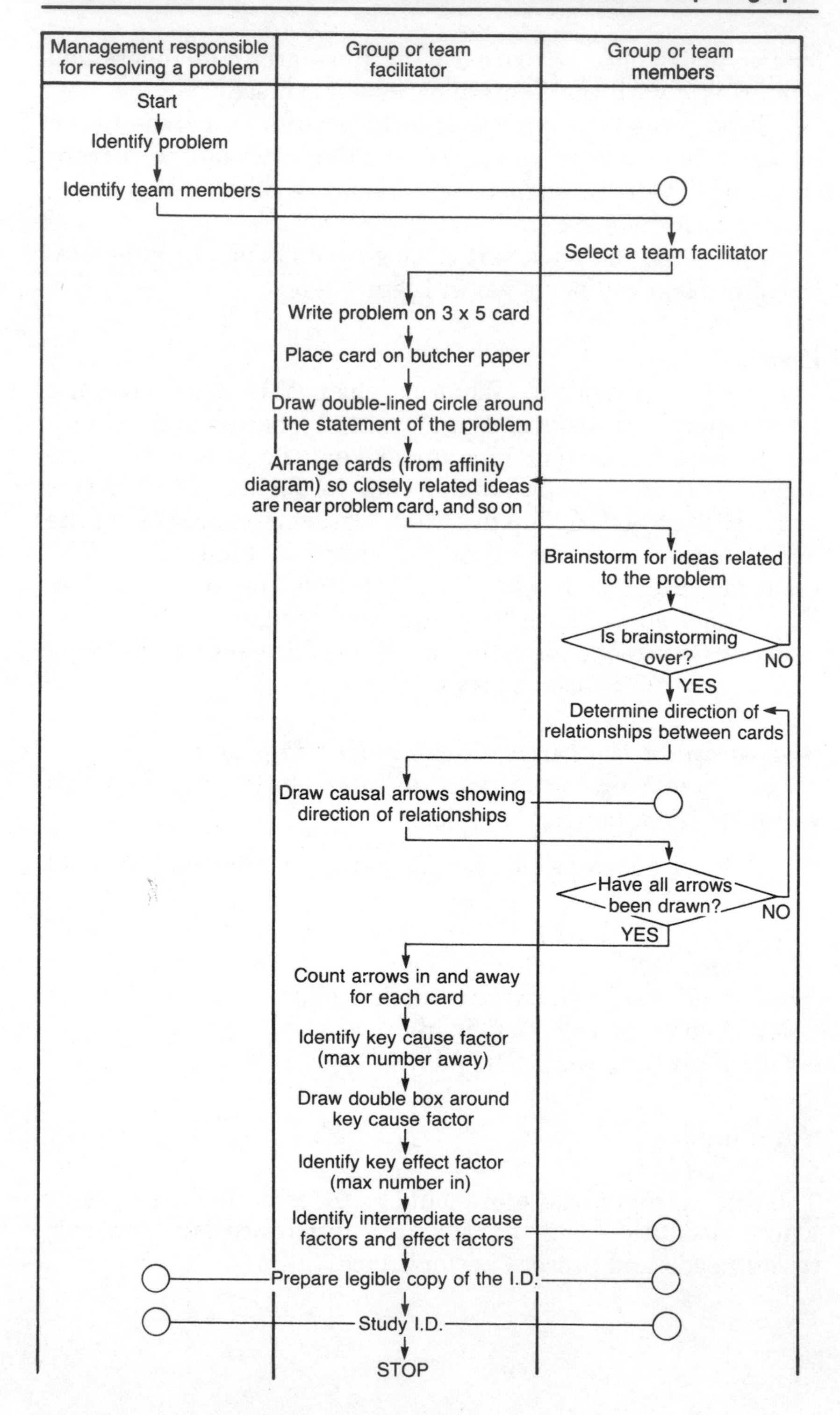

FIGURE 3–6
Interrelationship Diagraph—What Are the Problems in Achieving a Total Quality Transformation?

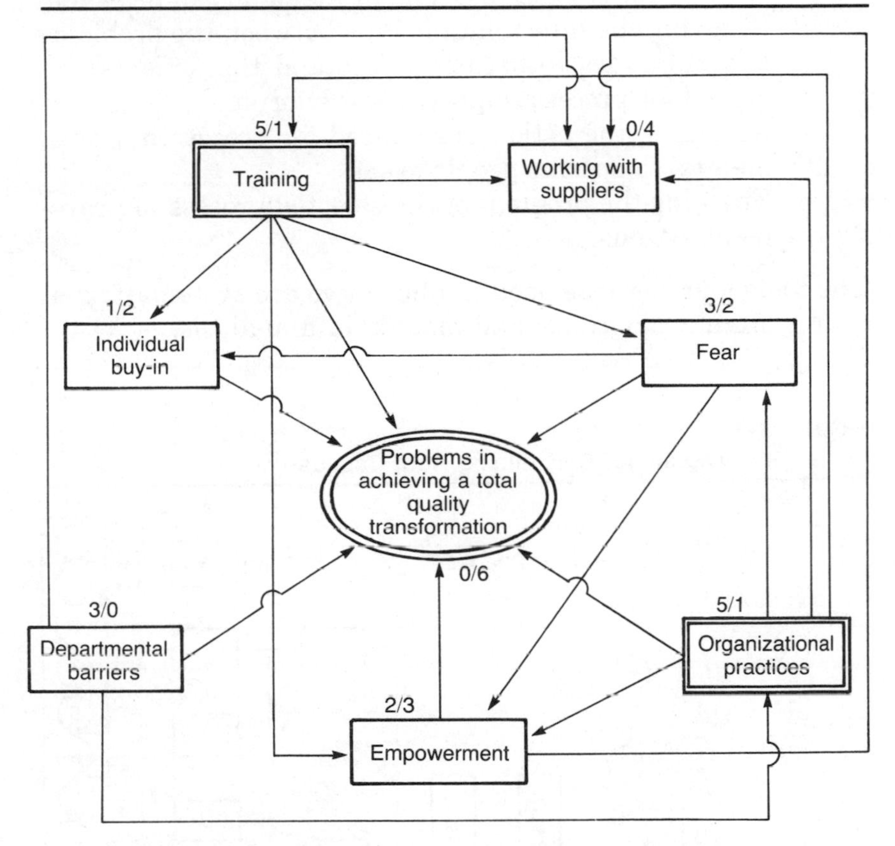

PHASE TWO: DETERMINING THE ACTIONS NEEDED TO RESOLVE THE PRODUCT OR PROCESS PROBLEMS DISCOVERED IN PHASE ONE

Introduction

Phase two centers on how to select the action(s) and resources required to resolve the product or process problems determined in phase one. The tools and methods utilized in this phase have four basic functions:

1. Systematically breaking down the problem(s) discovered in phase one until a list of subissues emerges on which process improvement action(s) can be taken.
2. Studying the interrelationships between the problems and subissues to better understand the action(s) required for process improvement efforts.
3. Assigning the action(s) required for process improvement(s) to specific people/areas.
4. Tracking the progress of the selected process improvement actions.

The tools and methods used in phase two are systematic diagrams, matrix diagrams, and matrix data analysis.

FIGURE 3–7
Systematic Diagram for Determining Root Causes

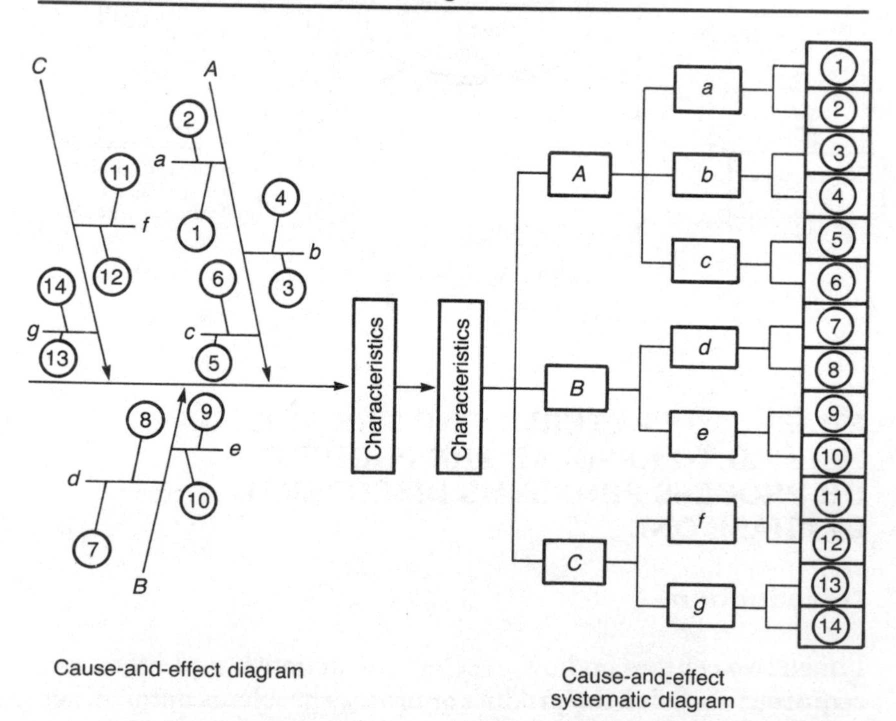

A cause-and-effect diagram and a cause-and-effect systematic diagram.

Source: Shigeru Mizuno, *Management for Quality Improvement: The 7 New QC Tools* (Cambridge, Mass.: Productivity Press, 1988), p. 158.

FIGURE 3–8
Systematic Diagram for Showing Means to Objectives

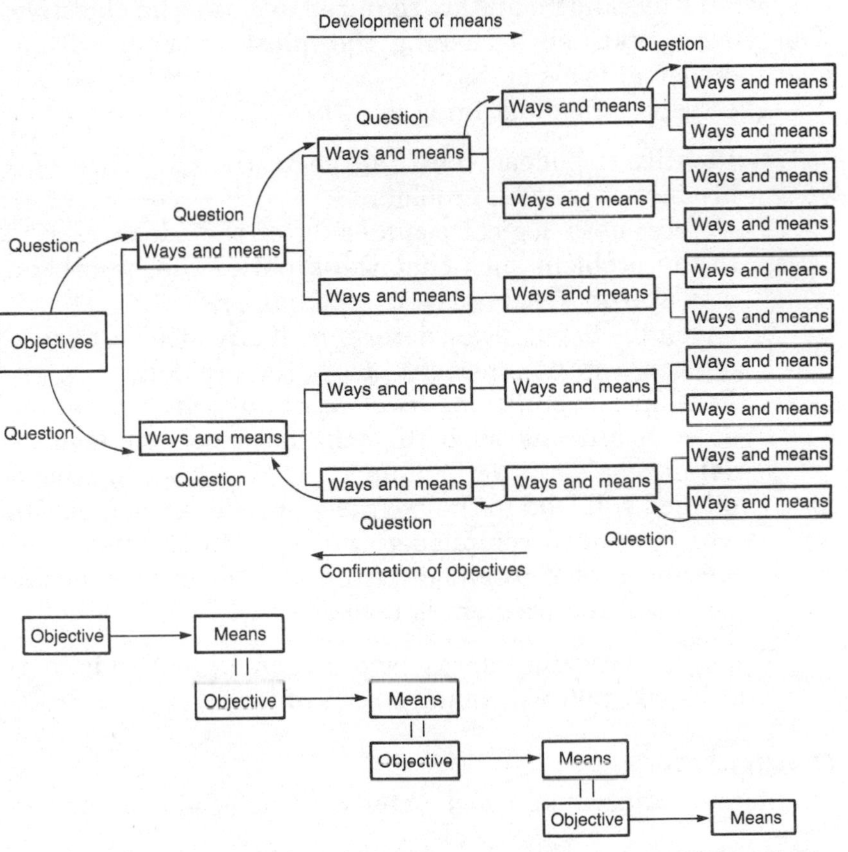

Source: Shigeru Mizuno, *Management for Quality Improvement: The 7 New QC Tools* (Cambridge, Mass.: Productivity Press, 1988), p. 149.

Systematic Diagram

A systematic diagram, also called a dendrogram or tree diagram, can be used to determine the root cause(s) of a problem or to generate a plan for solving a problem (determine the most effective means of accomplishing an objective). Figure 3–7 shows a systematic diagram for determining the root cause(s) of a problem. The systematic diagram in Figure 3–7 adds sequencing to a cause-and-effect diagram; that is, to accomplish A, a, b, and c must occur, and to accomplish a, 1 and 2 must occur, and so on. Figure 3–8 shows a systematic diagram to determine the most effective means of accomplishing an objective. This type of systematic diagram sequentially asks what ways and means are required to pursue an objective. This is accomplished by asking the question repeatedly at ever-increasing levels of detail.

The systematic diagram is used to:

1. Identify the ideas contributing to the existence of a product or process problem.
2. Determine a logical sequencing of the ideas related to the problem such that the problem can be broken into ever-increasing levels of detail.
3. Given the list of ideas, determine if any ideas are missing that can help better explain the problem.
4. Establish a sufficient level of detail when breaking down a problem such that the most specific level of detail represents actionable items, which when accomplished will lead to the next less specific level of detail, which when accomplished will lead to the next less specific level of detail, and so on. This process is continued until the problem is resolved.

The systematic diagram is useful when a problem is complex and its solution will require a lot of time.

Construction

A systematic diagram is constructed using the following procedure.

1. Management selects a problem.

2. Four or five people form a team to study the problem. Team members represent many different perspectives. Team members must agree on a clear and uncomplicated statement of the problem.

3. The team selects a facilitator to coordinate its activities.

4. Team members brainstorm a list of ideas that may aid in understanding the problem. The facilitator writes each idea on a 3 × 5 card or Post-it™ Note. The following suggestions may be helpful when brainstorming to construct a systematic diagram.

a. If an affinity diagram has already been constructed for the problem, team members use the affinity diagram cards as a starting point for brainstorming, but continue to brainstorm for new ideas.

b. If an interrelationship diagraph has already been constructed for the problem, team members use the idea cards as a starting point for brainstorming, but continue to brainstorm for new ideas. Team members use the sequential relationships indicated by the arrows on the interrelationship diagraph when ordering the cards on a systematic diagram. These sequential relationships will be extremely helpful in constructing the systematic diagram.

5. The team evaluates each suggested idea with one of the following codes:

(O) indicates an actionable idea.

(Δ) indicates an idea that requires more information to determine whether it is an actionable idea.

(X) indicates an unactionable idea. An X should be used only after carefully studying that all the possible alternatives for implementing the idea have been exhausted. Do not use an X hastily.

These code assignments will be helpful when constructing the systematic diagram.

6. The team constructs the systematic diagram by:

a. Placing the problem card on the left side of a work surface, such as a large conference table.

b. Locating the cards with ideas most closely related to the problem card by asking questions such as:

"______ must happen to achieve ______."

"______ causes ______."

c. Brainstorming for new ideas if no ideas exist that explain an idea card already on the systematic diagram, having the facilitator write these ideas on cards, and placing them on the systematic diagram where the team agrees.

d. Placing the idea cards selected in step *b* to the right of the problem card in a tree diagram fashion. The idea cards should be assembled so the ideas most related to the problem under study are to the immediate right of the problem card. Careful consideration of the means to an objective or the causes of an effect are the most important part of constructing a systematic diagram.

e. Repeating the procedure in step *d* for each of the "right-most" idea cards by asking questions such as:

"_______ must happen to achieve _______."
"_______ causes _______."

Continue this process until all idea cards are placed on the systematic diagram.

7. The team studies the systematic diagram. If there are gaps in the systematic diagram, team members brainstorm to close the gaps. The team continues to brainstorm to close any gaps in the systematic diagram for as long as is necessary to create a complete path between the problem under study and ideas that are specific enough to be action items that will resolve the problem.

Figure 3–9 shows an integrated flowchart of how to construct a systematic diagram.

Example

Recall the affinity diagram in Figure 3–4 concerning: "What are the problems in achieving a total quality transformation?" Suppose the team studying this question decides to focus on training. The team identified four main subideas relating to training: (1) structure, (2) instructor, (3) participant, and (4) environment. Figure 3–10 shows the results of the team trying to expand the subissue of environment. The sub-subissues are:

1. Before.
2. During.
3. After.

Next, the team expanded "during," which led to "external" and "internal." Finally, the team expanded "external" to "work

FIGURE 3–9
Integrated Flowchart of How to Construct a Systematic Diagram

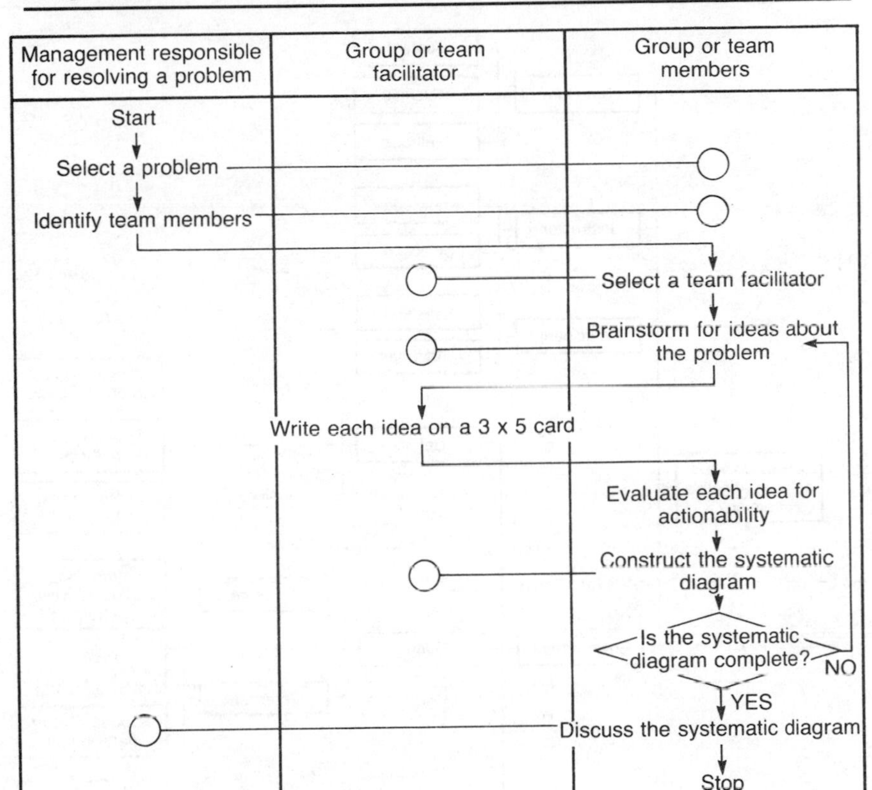

load adjusted while in training"; this is an actionable item. The level of detail in Figure 3–10 is extended until actionable items are determined, which, if accomplished, will result in a total quality transformation.

Workshop on the Systematic Diagram

Team members preparing to construct a systematic diagram will need the following supplies:

1. Five packages of 3 × 5 cards or five packages of 3 × 4 Post-it™ Notes.
2. One flip chart leader.

FIGURE 3–10
Systematic Diagram of How to Achieve Effective Training

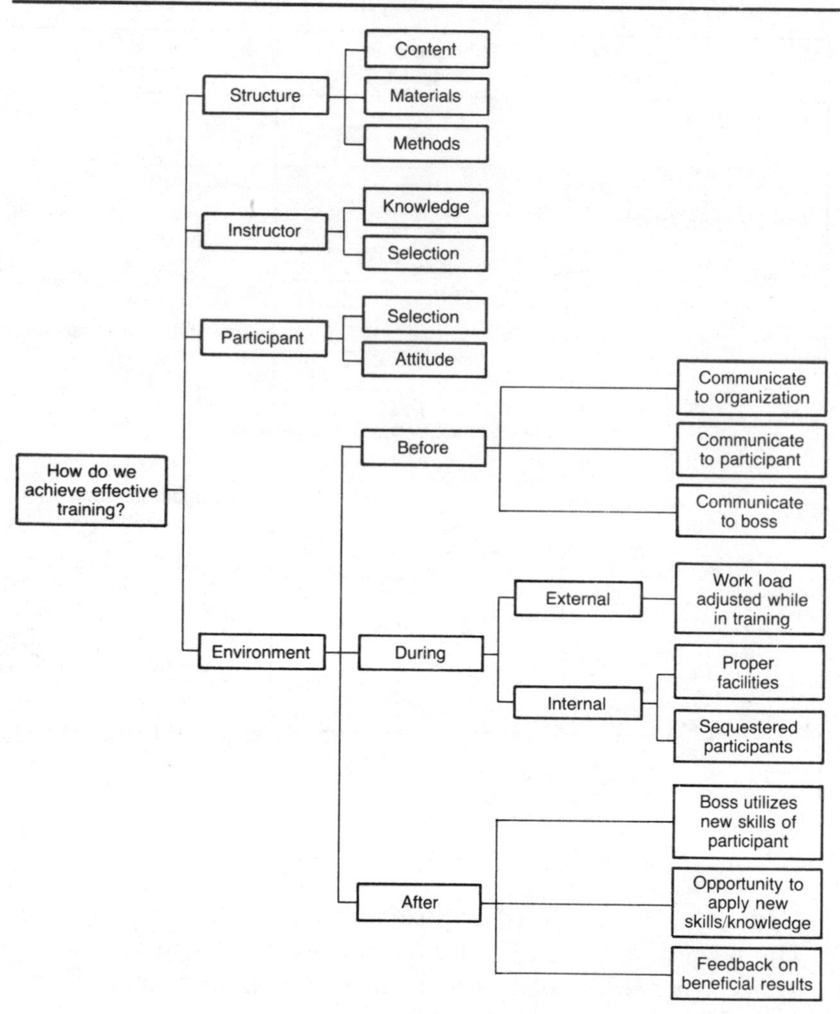

3. One roll of butcher paper.
4. One scissor to cut the butcher paper.
5. Pens (one per participant).
6. Pads (one per participant).
7. One ruler.

Matrix Diagram

The matrix diagram is often used to arrange large quantities of data relating to two or more product or process problems. The matrix diagram helps management locate and plug any holes in the information base relating to the problems.

There are several types of matrix diagrams, and the diagram's purpose determines the type used. The L-shaped and T-shaped matrix diagrams will be discussed in detail.

L-Shaped Matrix Diagram

The L-shaped matrix diagram, an uncomplicated, two-dimensional chart, explains the interrelationships between two product or process variables in a column and row (matrix) format. The columns represent the subcategories of one variable; the rows represent the subcategories of a second variable. In the matrix diagram, a variable can indicate almost anything; for example, the actions emanating out of a systematic diagram or a listing of items (people, departments, courses). The resulting matrix cells symbolize possible correlations between the subideas of the two problems. Figure 3–11 shows a generic L-shaped matrix diagram.

Figure 3–12 shows a series of L-shaped matrix diagrams that depict the interrelationships between customer needs and product features, product features and process features, and process features and process control features. These diagrams form part of an analysis known as quality function deployment.

Figure 3–13 illustrates the use of part of a systematic diagram in an L-shaped matrix diagram showing the interrelationships between "how to achieve effective training" and organizational areas/individuals.

T-Shaped Matrix Diagram

The T-shaped matrix diagram can be used to compare, correlate, or study two problems with respect to a third problem. Figure 3–14 shows a T-shaped matrix diagram that combines two L-shaped matrix diagrams. A common application of the T-matrix is to pinpoint training requirements, as shown in Figure 3–15.

FIGURE 3–11
Generic L-Shaped Matrix Diagram

A \ B	b_1	b_2	••••••	b_j	••••••	b_m
a_1						
a_2						
••••••						
a_i						
••••••						
a_n						

At the intersection, existence and strength of relation are examined and grasped.

Source: Kaoru Ishikawa, "Reports of Statistical Application Research, Union of Japanese Scientists and Engineers," *Reports of Statistical Application Research, JUSE* 33, no. 2 (June 1986), p. 14.

Construction

Matrix diagrams should be constructed in the following manner:

1. Select a problem.
2. Form a team consisting of four or five people. The team should identify the problems whose interrelationships are to be studied using the matrix diagram.
3. Select a facilitator to coordinate the team's activities.
4. Determine the product or process variables to be studied.
5. Decide on the matrix format, for example, the L-shaped or T-shaped matrix. Specify the detail for each product or process variable. The right-most level of detail on a systematic diagram would form the columns of a matrix diagram studying the relationship between the

FIGURE 3–12
L-Shaped Matrix Diagrams for Quality Function Deployment

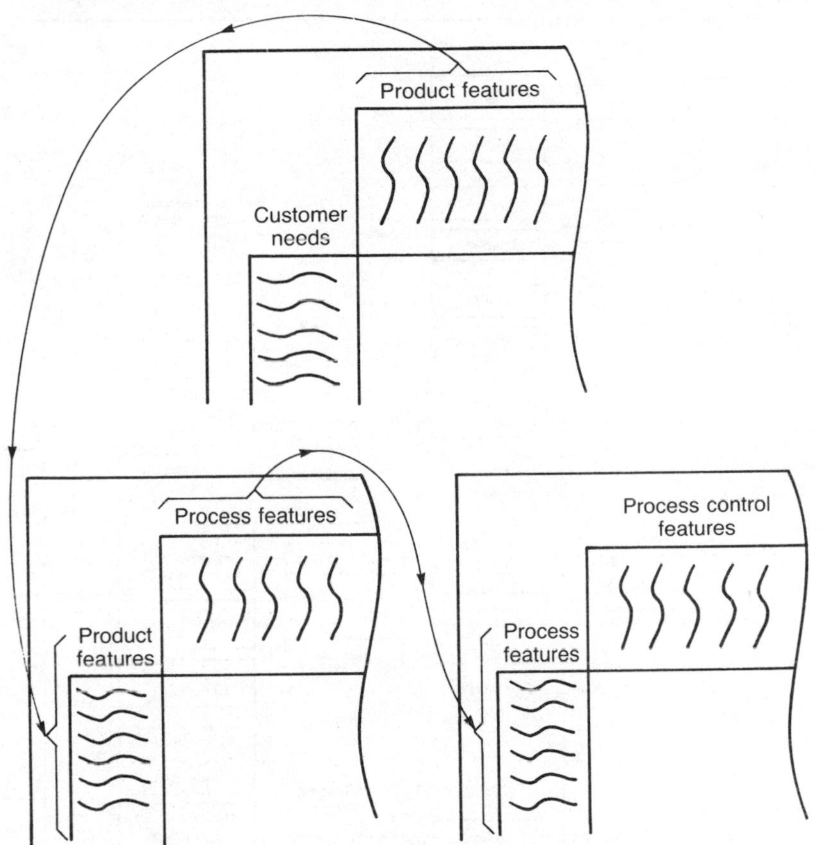

Source: Joseph Juran, *Juran on Leadership for Quality: An Executive Handbook* (New York: Free Press, 1989), p. 119.

problem statement from the systematic diagram and another product or process variable which would form the rows of the matrix diagram (see Figure 3–13).

6. Place the details of the problems on the matrix diagram so they form the axes of the matrix. This can be done by either positioning the cards (for example, the right-most level of detail on a systematic diagram) on butcher paper or recording the ideas directly on a flip chart. Given the trial-and-error nature of developing a matrix, cards are easier to shift around.
7. Draw in the lines of the matrix.

FIGURE 3–13
L-Shaped Matrix Diagram Example—How Do We Achieve Effective Training?

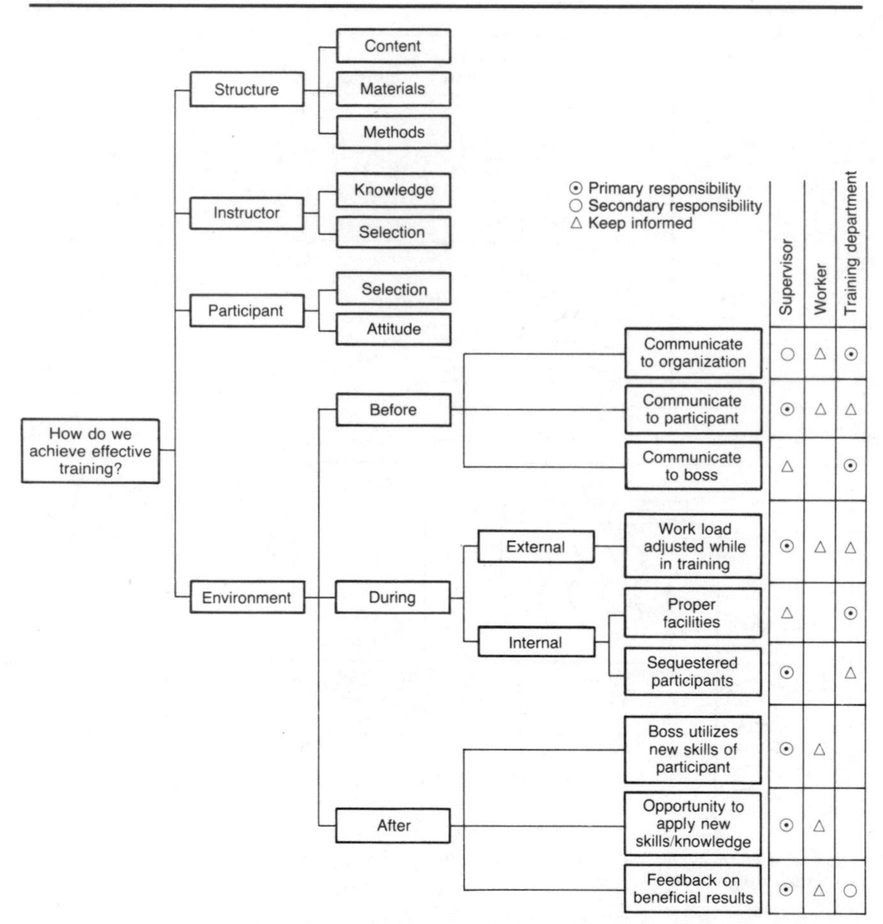

8. Determine the symbols to be utilized to illustrate relationships. Be sure to include a description (legend) of the symbols on the matrix diagram. The most common symbols used to depict functional responsibilities are:

(⊙) Primary responsibility

(○) Secondary responsibility

(△) Keep informed

The most common symbols used to depict the relationships between quality characteristics are:

(⊙) Extremely important

(○) Very important

(△) Important

9. Enter the appropriate symbol into each cell of the matrix diagram. The symbol should denote the nature

FIGURE 3–14
T-Shaped Matrix Diagram

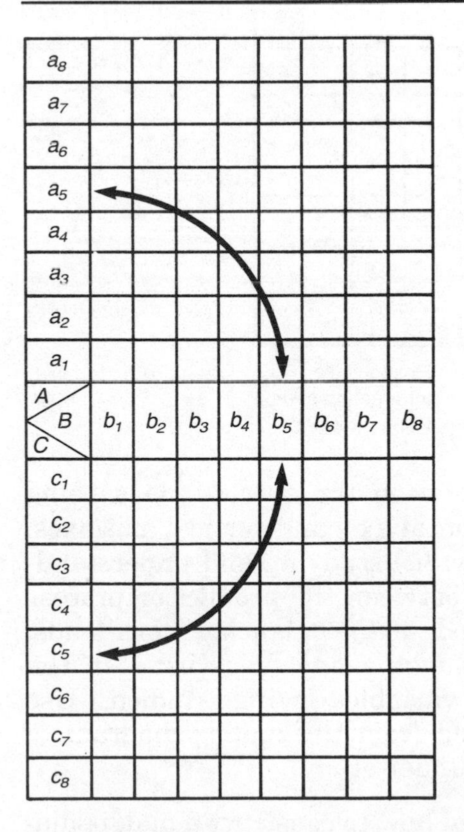

Source: Kaoru Ishikawa, "Reports of Statistical Application Research, Union of Japanese Scientists and Engineers," *Reports of Statistical Application Research, JUSE* 33, no. 2 (June 1986), p. 15.

FIGURE 3–15
T-Shaped Matrix Diagram for Training

TO: Organization	TO: Participant	TO: Boss	Training needs: What needs to be communicated (2 way)	FROM: Training coordinator	FROM: Steering committee	FROM: Boss	FROM: Instructor/S.M.E.
	△	△	Prerequisites	⊙	△		○
△	△	△	Objectives of course	○	△	⊙	
△	△	△	Objectives of big picture		⊙		
△	△	△	Where this course "fits"		⊙		
△	△	△	Who should attend	○	△	⊙	
△	△	△	Benefits		⊙		○
	△	△	Topics/content	⊙	△		○
	△	△	When	⊙			
	△	△	Where	⊙			
	△	△	How long	⊙			
△	△	△	Effect on job		○	⊙	○

⊙ = Responsible
○ = Information source
△ = Keep informed

of the relationship between the specific ideas being analyzed on the horizontal axis and vertical axis/axes.

10. Analyze the matrix by: (*a*) studying and understanding the relationships between the product or process variables being studied, or (*b*) balancing work loads, or (*c*) locating and plugging any holes between the product or process variables being studied. Use the information gained from the matrix diagram to resolve the problems under study.

An integrated flowchart of how to construct a matrix diagram is shown in Figure 3–16.

FIGURE 3–16
Integrated Flowchart of How to Construct a Matrix Diagram

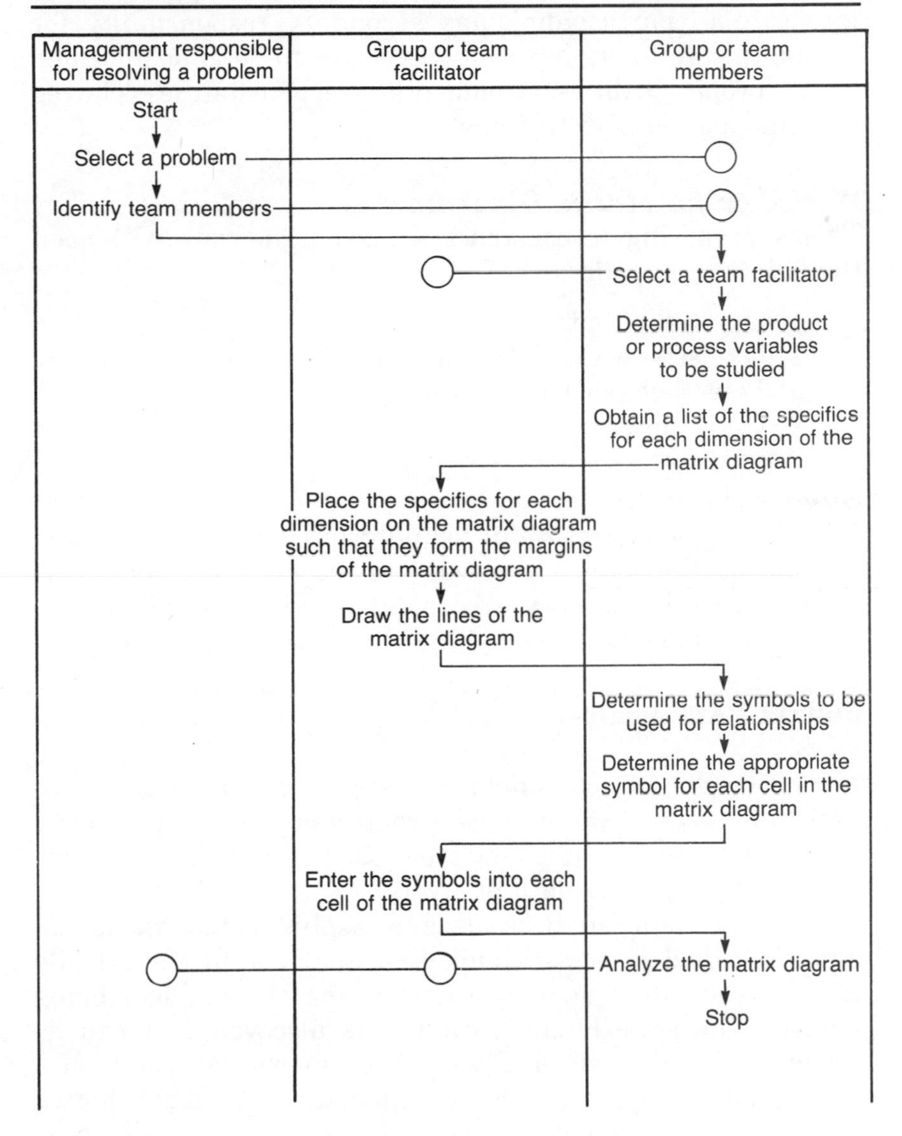

Example

Figure 3–13 shows an L-shaped matrix using the systematic diagram for "How do we achieve effective training?" as the vertical axis and the people needed to resolve the training problem as the horizontal axis. For example, Figure 3–13 shows that the supervisor has primary responsibility for "communicate to participant," has secondary responsibility for "communicate to organization," and has to be kept informed about "proper facilities," among other responsibilities relating to achieving effective training.

Workshop for Matrix Diagram

Teams preparing to construct a matrix diagram will need the following supplies:

1. One roll of butcher paper.
2. One scissor to cut the butcher paper.
3. Pens (one per participant).
4. One ruler.

Summary

Matrix diagrams are useful for determining, assigning, and monitoring the actions necessary to resolve a problem. This method provides an easy way for identifying the individuals and/or departments responsible for resolving a problem.

Matrix Data Analysis

If a matrix diagram does not adequately explain the interrelationships among two or more product or process problems, deeper study is required. One tool used to study these interrelationships is matrix data analysis.

Matrix data analysis uses a sophisticated statistical method, called principle component analysis, to statistically identify the latent structure underlying the problem being studied. Once the latent structure is discovered, it can be understood and resolved. Figure 3–17 shows the results of a matrix data analysis (principle components analysis) to better understand food item preference categories in Japan. Further discussion of this tool is not offered here because it requires a significant background in statistical theory. Instead, we will discuss two related and simpler tools, a perceptual map and a glyph.

FIGURE 3–17
Matrix Data Analysis of Food Item Preference Categories

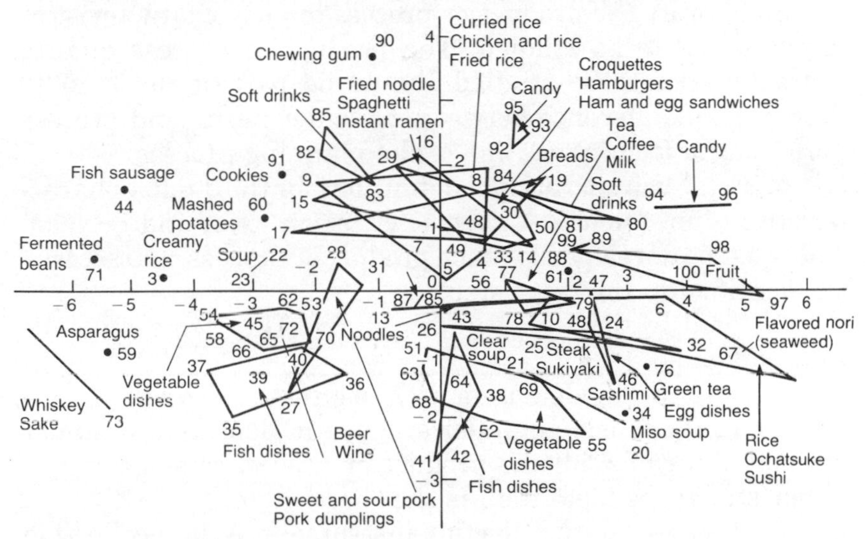

Source: Shigeru Mizuno, *Management for Quality Improvement: The 7 New QC Tools* (Cambridge, Mass.: Productivity Press, 1988), p. 206.

Perceptual Map

A perceptual map helps to understand the interrelationships between two or more items with respect to product or process quality characteristics (called dimensions). For example, suppose a raw material with 10 quality characteristics is purchased from five suppliers. In this case, the 10 quality characteristics form the dimensions of a 10-dimensional space and the five suppliers are the items in the 10-dimensional space. A perceptual map could highlight the similarities and dissimilarities between the five suppliers with respect to the 10 quality characteristics. For example, groupings of bad and good suppliers might emerge, helping clarify relationships between product or process problems that bear on process improvement.

Construction

Constructing and analyzing a perceptual map requires the following steps.

1. Decide on a problem to solve.

2. Determine if a perceptual map is the appropriate tool.

3. Identify the product or process quality characteristics (dimensions) to be studied. The product or process quality characteristics to be studied should be part of the plan to decrease the difference between customer needs and process performance from phase one of the planning process.

4. Establish operational definitions for the quality characteristics (dimensions). A specific criterion, test, and decision rule must be developed for each product or process characteristic identified in the prior step.

5. Identify the items under study. The items must be clearly defined.

6. Describe an ideal item with respect to the quality characteristics (dimensions) under study. An ideal item assumes optimal values for all the product or process characteristics under study; the ideal item is the "best" item.

7. Prepare a data collection instrument. A data collection form must be developed to collect information about the various items under study and the ideal item, with respect to the quality characteristics (dimensions) under study. Figure 3–18 shows an example of a data collection instrument for a perceptual map concerning the quality characteristics of wood chips delivered to a paper mill from its suppliers.

8. Pretest the data collection instrument. Make sure the instrument is capable of collecting the desired data; for example:

a. Does the data collection instrument contain any words unfamiliar to the respondent or data collector?

b. Does the data collection instrument lead the respondent to give inaccurate answers?

c. Does the data collection instrument contain double questions? (Do you like Fords and Nissans?)

9. Determine the sampling plan for collecting data. It is important to determine if information about the items under study will be collected from:

- One source at one point in time.
- Multiple sources at one point in time.

FIGURE 3–18
Record of Wood Chip Supplier Quality by Supplier (To be completed by the buyer's receiving department)

Supplier Number	*Date*	*Percentage of Fines*	*Percentage of Overs*	*Percentage of Thick*	*Percentage of Bark*
•					
• Insert data as they become available from the buyer's receiving department.					
•					

Legend: Date = delivery date of carload of wood chips.
Percentage of fines = percentage of carload that is sawdust.
Percentage of overs = percentage of cardload that is over-sized wood chips.
Percentage of thick = percentage of carload that is over-thick wood chips.
Percentage of bark = percentage of carload that is bark.

Note: The above data must be studied to determine the stability of percentage of fines, percentage of overs, percentage of thick, or percentage of bark for each supplier's process.

If each supplier's process is stable with respect to each of the above variables, and will remain so in the opinion of an expert, then the averages can be used to estimate what each supplier will deliver in the future and the perceptual map will be useful in developing a plan on how to improve the quality of incoming wood chips.

However, if each supplier's process is not stable with respect to one or more of the above variables, then the averages cannot be used to estimate what each supplier will deliver in the future and the perceptual map will be of limited value in developing a plan on how to improve the quality of incoming wood chips.

As always, if one or more variables and/or suppliers are not stable, then these processes must be stabilized. Stabilizing a process gives it an identity, a known capability. A process without an identity cannot be improved.

- One source at multiple points in time.
- Multiple sources at multiple points in time.

The above determination makes it clear whether the data to be analyzed consist of single values or averages. If multiple sources and/or multiple points in time are to be used, a sampling plan must be specified to collect the data. The sampling plan must conform to the standards of statistical practice.

The data should be collected in rigid accordance with the sampling plan.

10. Collect the data in accordance with the established sampling plan.

11. Place the collected data onto a matrix diagram. The data must be inserted onto a matrix diagram whose rows are represented by the items under study, including the ideal item, and whose columns are represented by the quality characteristics (dimensions) under study. The numeric values that go into any cell in the matrix diagram are either individual values or averages. Figure 3–19 shows a matrix diagram constructed from the data collected using the wood chip data collection instrument shown in Figure 3–18.

12. Calculate the distance measures between items. Similarities between items, including the ideal item, can be studied by calculating the distance between items on the perceptual map. The measure of distance on a perceptual map, called a

FIGURE 3–19
Geometric Averages of Wood Chip Quality by Supplier for the Month of ________, 19XX

Each month the geometric averages for percentage of fines, percentage of overs, percentage of thick, and percentage of bark are computed for each supplier and inserted onto Figure 3–19. Hence, Figure 3–19 contains geometric averages by supplier number (rows) and percentage of carload with a given type of defect (columns).

Supplier Number	*Percentage of Fines*	*Percentage of Overs*	*Percentage of Thick*	*Percentage of Bark*
1	8	7	5	13
2	7	6	6	15
3	5	9	4	9
4	9	5	3	2
5	3	2	2	2
Ideal	0	0	0	0

For example, 15% is the value of item 2 (a month's worth of carloads filled with wood chips from supplier 2) on product or process characteristic 4 (geometric average percent of supplier 2's carloads, by weight, that are bark).

Minkowski metric, is the multivariate version of Euclidean distance.

It is very easy to compute the Minkowski metric between any two items, say item i and item j. Simply subtract item i's score from item j's score for each dimension and add the differences. The sum of these differences is the Minkowski metric of the distance between item i and item j, called D_{ij}. The formula for computing a Minkowski metric is:

$$D_{ij} = \Sigma_{h=1}^{k} |X_{ih} - X_{jh}|$$

where

X_{ih} = the measurement for item i on product or process characteristic h,

X_{jh} = the measurement for item j on product or process characteristic h, and

k = the number of product or process characteristics (items) under study.

Figure 3–20 shows the Minkowski metric distances between all pairs of items in the four-dimensional space shown in Figure 3–19.

13. Analyze the distance measures for all pairs of items. Common practice would lead to a study of the distances between all pairs of items on the perceptual map, including the ideal item. If a distance is small, then the items or dimensions are viewed as being similar; the opposite is true if the distances are large. Items close to the ideal item are viewed as possessing positive product or process characteristic traits, while the opposite holds true for items far from the ideal item. The clustering of items and the location of item clusters with respect to the ideal item may spur possible countermeasures for resolving problems.

Proper analysis requires avoiding the tendency to rank order distances; that is, assuming the largest distance represents the two most dissimilar items or, conversely, the smallest distance represents the two most similar items.

A correct analysis of the distances requires a study of the causes of variation among the distances. If all variation among distances can be explained by system causes, then all distances should be treated equally and no special counter-

FIGURE 3–20
Item Distance Matrix

Supplier Number	*1*	*2*	*3*	*4*	*5*	*Ideal*
1	X	5	10	26	24	33
2	X	X	13	19	25	34
3	X	X	X	16	18	27
4	X	X	X	X	10	19
5	X	X	X	X	X	9
Ideal	X	X	X	X	X	X

For example, the distance between supplier 1 and supplier 2 is (8 − 7) + (7 − 6) + (5 − 6) + (13 − 15) = 5.
The distance between supplier 3 and the ideal supplier is (5 − 0) + (9 − 0) + (4 − 0) + (9 − 0) = 27.

The prior analysis assumes all suppliers had an equal opportunity to produce percentage of fines, percentage of overs, percentage of thick, and percentage of bark for the month under study.

A control chart of the distances between the ideal supplier and all other suppliers revealed that supplier 5 is out of control; supplier 5 is a special supplier. Perhaps the wood chip process for all suppliers can be improved by studying supplier 5's process.

Upper control limit = 39.2.
Center line = 122/5 = 24.4.
Lower control limit = 9.6 (hence, 9 or less is out of control).

measure should be taken based on the size of any distance, such as the largest or smallest distances. However, if any variation among distances can be attributed to special causes of variation, then the distances should be studied to establish countermeasures that will move one or more items toward the ideal item. Figure 3–20 illustrates this.

Assumptions

All information drawn from a perceptual map assumes:

1. It is possible to operationally define the quality characteristics (dimensions) under study.
2. The dimensions are independent of each other.

3. The dimensions are equally important to the problem under study.
4. It is possible to locate all items with respect to the dimensions under study.
5. It is possible to describe an ideal item with respect to the dimensions under study.
6. The distribution of items for each dimension symmetrically decreases in all directions from the ideal item.

An integrated flowchart of how to construct a perceptual map is shown in Figure 3–21.

Example

An example of a perceptual map comparing various brands of beer with respect to two customer quality characteristics (mildness and lightness) is shown in Figure 3–22.

Workshop on the Perceptual Map

A team preparing to construct a perceptual map will need the following supplies:

1. Flip chart.
2. Two different colored markers.
3. Pens (one per participant).
4. Pads (one per participant).

Glyph

A glyph, like a perceptual map, helps to reveal the interrelationships between two or more items with respect to product or process quality characteristics (called dimensions). Again, suppose a raw material with 10 quality characteristics is purchased from five suppliers. The 10 quality characteristics form the dimensions of a 10-dimensional glyph and the five suppliers are the items on the 10-dimensional glyph. As with the perceptual map, a glyph could highlight the similarities and dissimilarities between the five suppliers with respect to the 10 quality characteristics. For example, groupings of bad and good suppliers might clarify relationships between product or process problems that bear on process improvement.

FIGURE 3–21
Integrated Flowchart of How to Construct a Perceptual Map

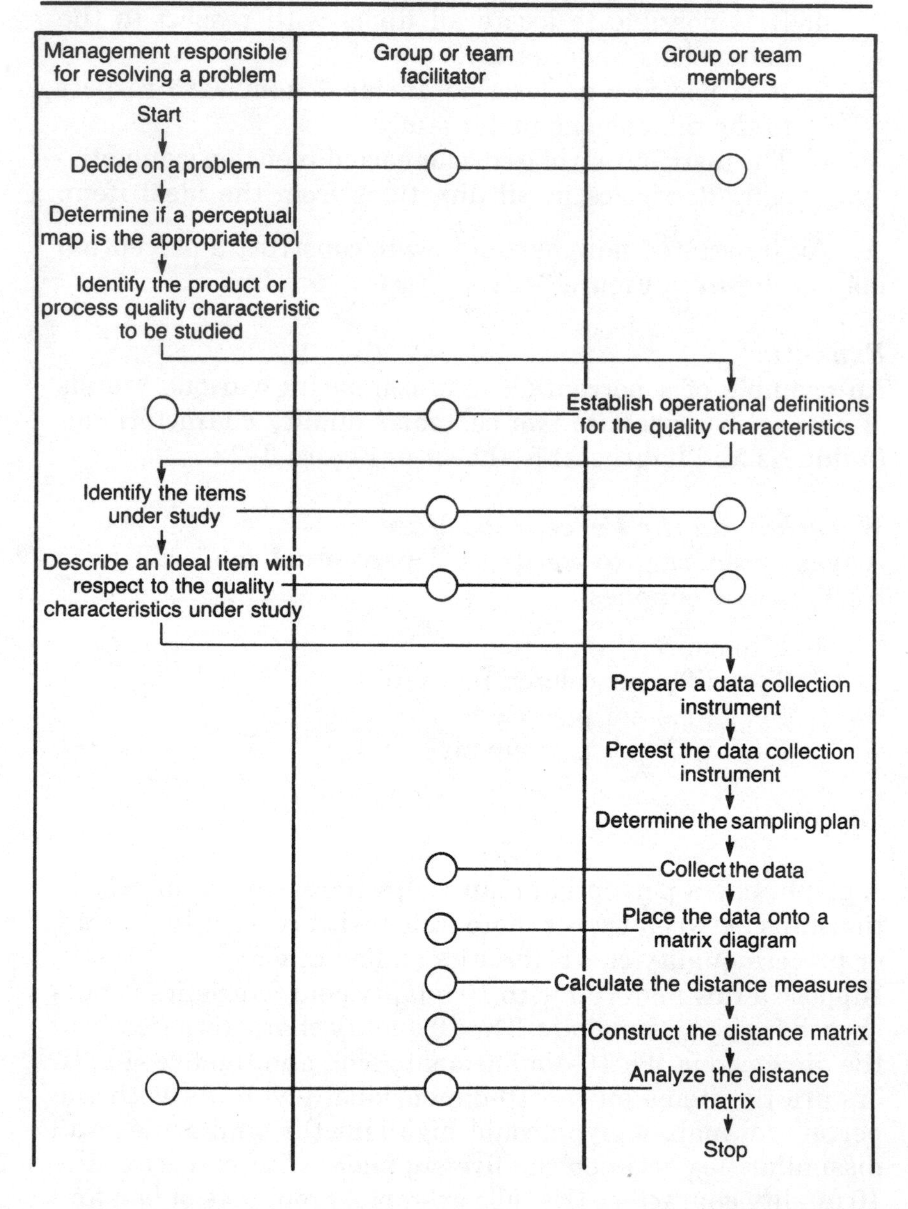

FIGURE 3–22
Perceptual Map for Beer Preferences

Distribution of consumer perceptions of beer brands according to mildness and lightness

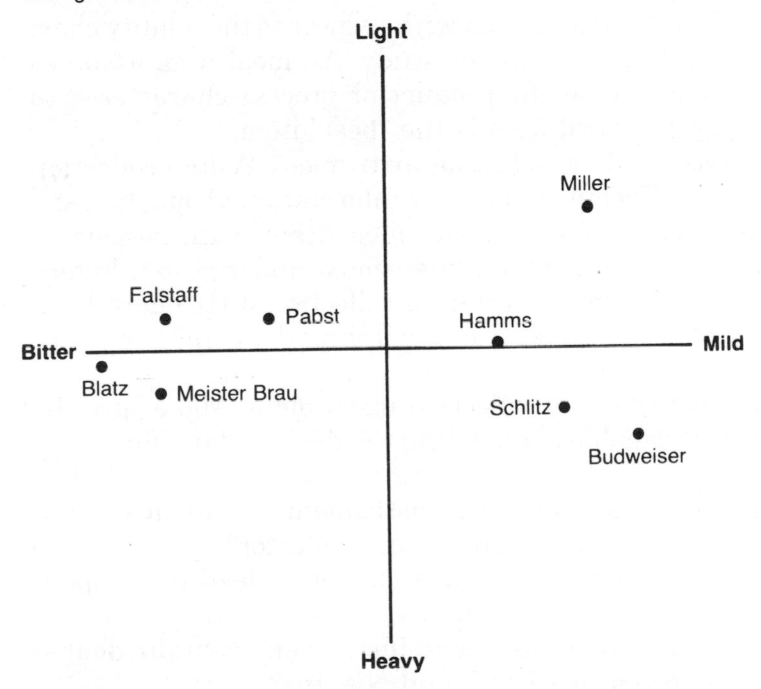

Source: Philip Kotler, *Marketing Models: A Model Building Approach* (New York: Holt, Rinehart & Winston, 1971), p. 493.

Construction and Example

Constructing and analyzing a glyph requires the following steps:

1. Decide on a problem to solve.

2. Determine if a glyph is the appropriate tool for the problem under study.

3. Identify the product or process quality characteristics (dimensions) to be studied. The product or process quality characteristics to be studied should be part of the plan to decrease the difference between customer needs and process performance from phase one of the planning process.

4. Establish operational definitions for the quality characteristics (dimensions). A specific criterion, test, and decision rule must be developed for each product or process characteristic identified in the prior step.

5. Identify the items under study. The items must be clearly defined.

6. Describe an ideal item with respect to the quality characteristics (dimensions) under study. An ideal item assumes optimal values for all the product or process characteristics under study; the ideal item is the "best" item.

7. Prepare a data collection instrument. A data collection form must be developed to collect information about the various items under study and the ideal item, with respect to the quality characteristics (dimensions) under study. Figure 3–23 shows an example of a data collection instrument for a glyph concerning the quality of wood chips delivered to a paper mill from its suppliers.

8. Pretest the data collection instrument. Make sure the instrument is capable of collecting the desired data; for example:

a. Does the data collection instrument contain any words unfamiliar to the respondent or data collector?

b. Does the data collection instrument lead the respondent to give inaccurate answers?

c. Does the data collection instrument contain double questions? (Do you like Fords and Nissans?)

9. Determine the sampling plan for collecting data. It is important to determine if information about the items under study will be collected from:

- One source at one point in time.
- Multiple sources at one point in time.
- One source at multiple points in time.
- Multiple sources at multiple points in time.

The above determination makes it clear whether the data to be analyzed consist of single values or averages. If multiple sources and/or multiple points in time are to be used, a sampling plan must be specified to collect the data. The sampling plan must conform to the standards of statistical practice. The data should be collected in rigid accordance with the sampling plan.

FIGURE 3–23
Record of Wood Chip Supplier Quality by Supplier (to be completed by the buyer's receiving department)

Supplier Number	*Date*	*Percentage of Fines*	*Percentage of Overs*	*Percentage of Thick*	*Percentage of Bark*
•					
• Insert data as they become available from the buyer's receiving department.					
•					

Legend: Date = delivery date of carload of wood chips.
Percentage of fines = percentage of carload that is sawdust.
Percentage of overs = percentage of carload that is over-sized wood chips.
Percentage of thick = percentage of carload that is over-thick wood chips.
Percentage of bark = percentage of carload that is bark.

Note: The above data must be studied to determine the stability of percentage of fines, percentage of overs, percentage of thick, or percentage of bark for each supplier's process.

If each supplier's process is stable with respect to each of the above variables, and will remain so in the opinion of an expert, then the averages can be used to estimate what each supplier will deliver in the future, and the glyph will be useful in developing a plan on how to improve the quality of incoming wood chips.

However, if each supplier's process is not stable with respect to one or more of the above variables, then the averages cannot be used to estimate what each supplier will deliver in the future, and the glyph will be of limited value in developing a plan on how to improve the quality of incoming wood chips.

As always, if one or more variables and/or suppliers are not stable, then these processes must be stabilized. Stabilizing a process gives it an identity, or a known capability. A process without an identity cannot be improved.

10. Collect the data in accordance with the established sampling plan.

11. Place the collected data onto a matrix diagram. The data must be inserted onto a matrix diagram whose rows are represented by the items under study, including the ideal item, and whose columns are represented by the quality characteristics (dimensions) under study. The numeric values that go into any cell in the matrix diagram are either individual values or averages.

12. Calculate the statistics for each item. Similarities between items, including the ideal item, can be studied by comparing the statistics for each item on the glyph. Figure 3–24 shows the statistics for a glyph concerning wood chip quality.

13. Plot the statistics for each quality characteristic, for each item, on the glyph. Figure 3–25 shows the glyph constructed from the geometric averages concerning wood chip quality shown in Figure 3–24.

14. Analyze the statistics for each item. Common practice would lead to a comparative study of the statistics for each item on the glyph, including the ideal item. If the difference between two items' statistics is small with respect to a particular quality characteristic, then the items are viewed as being similar; if the opposite is true, the difference between two statistics is large. Items whose glyphs are close to the ideal

FIGURE 3–24
Geometric Averages of Wood Chip Quality by Supplier for the Month of ______, 19XX

Each month, the geometric averages for percentage of fines, percentage of overs, percentage of thick, and percentage of bark are computed for each supplier and inserted onto Figure 3–24. Hence, Figure 3–24 contains geometric averages by supplier number (rows) and percentage of carloads with a given type of defect (columns).

Supplier Number	*Percentage of Fines*	*Percentage of Overs*	*Percentage of Thick*	*Percentage of Bark*
1	8	7	5	13
2	7	6	6	15
3	5	9	4	9
4	9	5	3	2
5	3	2	2	2
Ideal	0	0	0	0

For example, 15% is the value of item 2 (a month's worth of carloads filled with wood chips from supplier 2) on product or process characteristic 4 (geometric average percent of supplier 2's carloads, by weight, that are bark).

FIGURE 3–25
Glyph for Wood Chip Statistics

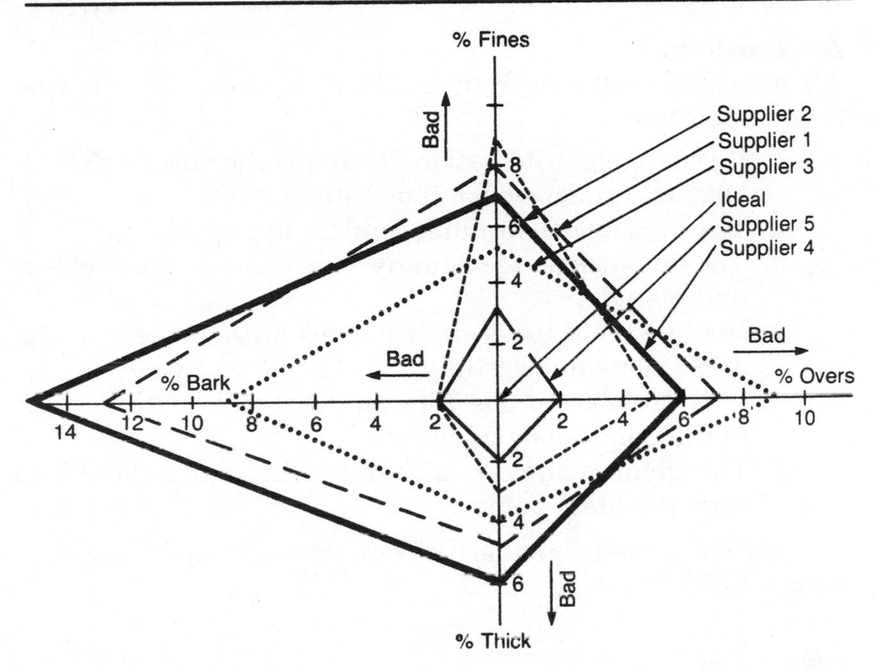

item's glyph are viewed as possessing positive product or process characteristic traits, while the opposite holds true for items whose glyphs are far from the ideal item. The location of an item's glyph with respect to the ideal item may spur possible countermeasures for resolving problems.

Proper analysis requires avoiding the tendency to rank order distances; that is, assuming the largest distance represents the two most dissimilar items or, conversely, the smallest distance represents the two most similar items.

A correct analysis of the distances requires a study of the causes of variation among the distances. If all variation among distances can be explained by system causes, then all distances should be treated equally and no special countermeasure should be taken based on the size of any distance, such as the largest or smallest distances. However, if any variation among distances can be attributed to special causes of variation, then the distances should be studied to establish countermeasures that will move one or more items toward the ideal item. Figure 3–26 illustrates this.

Assumptions

All information drawn from a glyph assumes the following conditions exist:

1. It is possible to operationally define the quality characteristics (dimensions) under study.
2. The dimensions are independent of each other.
3. The dimensions are equally important to the problem under study.
4. It is possible to locate all items with respect to the dimensions under study.
5. It is possible to describe an ideal item with respect to the dimensions under study.
6. The glyph symmetrically decreases in all directions from the ideal item.

An integrated flowchart of how to construct a glyph is shown in Figure 3–27.

FIGURE 3–26
Control Charts by Quality Characteristic without the Ideal Supplier Included in the Statistics

Percentage of Fines	*Percentage of Overs*	*Percentage of Thick*	*Percentage of Bark*
UCL = 14.0	UCL = 13.0	UCL = 10.0	UCL = 16.8
CL = 6.4	CL = 5.8	CL = 4.0	CL = 8.2
LCL = 0.0	LCL = 0.0	LCL = 0.0	LCL = 0.0
In control	In control	In control	In control

The prior analysis assumes all suppliers had an equal opportunity to produce percentage of fines, percentage of overs, percentage of thick, and percentage of bark for the month under study.

Note: This does not imply the suppliers are in control in a multidimensional sense; that is, simultaneously for all quality characteristics.

UCL = Upper control limit
CL = Center line
LCL = Lower control limit

FIGURE 3–27
Integrated Flowchart of How to Construct a Glyph

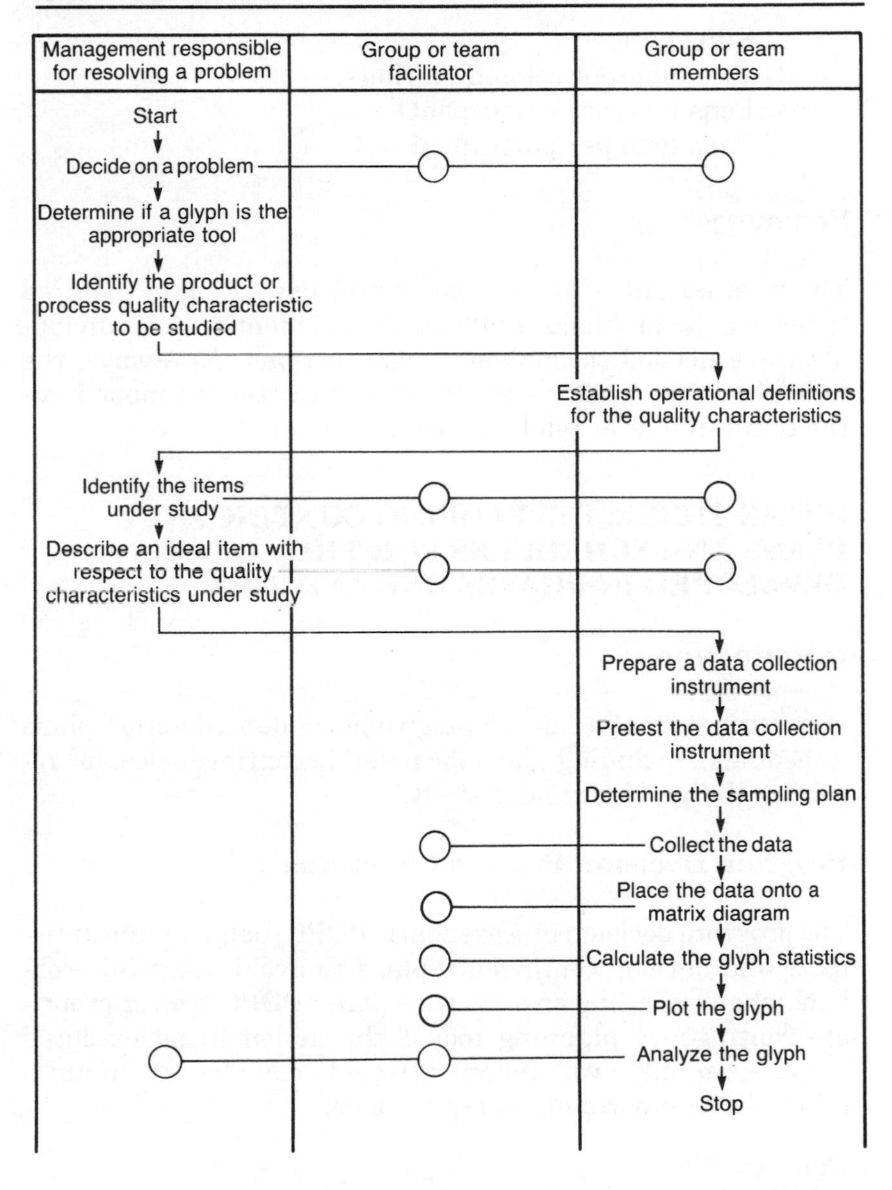

Workshop on the Glyph

A team constructing a glyph will need the following supplies:

1. Flip chart.
2. Two different colored markers.
3. Pens (one per participant).
4. Pads (one per participant).

Summary

The final output of phase two should list action(s) required to resolve the problems under study and identify the individuals/areas needed to implement said actions. As always, the individuals assigned to implement the action(s) must have the commitment of relevant process owners.

PHASE THREE: DEVELOPING CONTINGENCY PLANS AND SCHEDULES FOR THE ACTIONS DEVELOPED IN PHASES ONE AND TWO

Introduction

Phase three involves developing time-sequenced action plans (schedules), including plans for possible contingencies, for resolving the problem under study.

Program Decision Process Chart Analysis

The program decision process chart (PDPC) helps a team anticipate and develop contingency plans to avoid potential problems when executing an action in a plan.[2] PDPC is an appropriate contingency planning tool if the action to be executed requires an unknown amount of time to complete in an unfamiliar set of environmental conditions.

Construction

A PDPC is constructed using the following steps:

1. Select an action in need of a contingency plan.

2. Identify a team appropriate to solve the problem under study.

3. Select a facilitator to coordinate the team's activities.

4. Begin with a systematic diagram of the problem.

5. Select one branch from the systematic diagram relevant to the problem and brainstorm for the answers to the following two questions with respect to each "right-most" action item:

- What are the potential problems in accomplishing this action item?
- What contingency plans could be developed to avoid the potential problems?

Answering these questions will form the basis of a contingency plan for coping with potential problems. Don't be overwhelmed by the explosion of contingencies that will surface. Take the actions one at a time.

6. Record the information from the second question on a new branch to the right of the original branch. Enclose these contingencies in "clouds" (similar to cartoon captions). Draw arrows between the contingencies and the original action items indicating which original action items are affected by a particular contingency plan.

7. Continue steps 5 and 6 on the selected branch of the systematic diagram until brainstorming has been completed.

8. Repeat steps 5 and 6 for each remaining branch on the systematic diagram.

9. Assemble all branches into a final PDPC, review the PDPC, and modify and/or add to the action plan and contingency plans.

10. Analyze the PDPC.

A team doing contingency planning by using a PDPC analysis can follow the steps shown in the integrated flowchart in Figure 3–28.

Example

Figure 3–29 shows a PDPC analysis developed for "What could happen to cause an unsuccessful training experience?" The contingency plan to deal with the branch "What could go wrong in class"—"Equipment" failure—"Bulb blows" is to have a "spare" bulb on hand.

FIGURE 3–28
Integrated Flowchart of How to Construct a PDPC

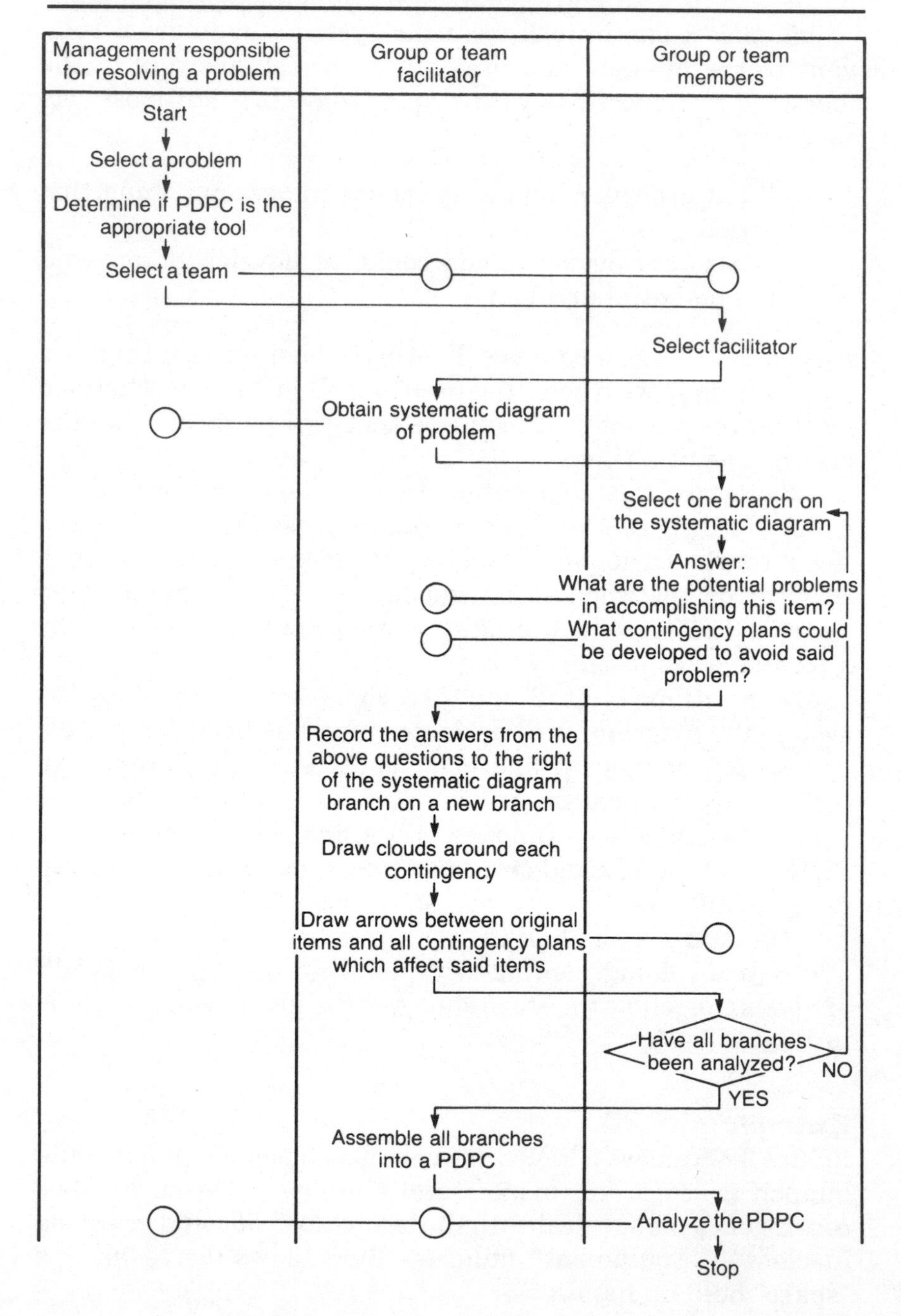

FIGURE 3–29
What Could Happen to Cause an Unsuccessful Training Experience?

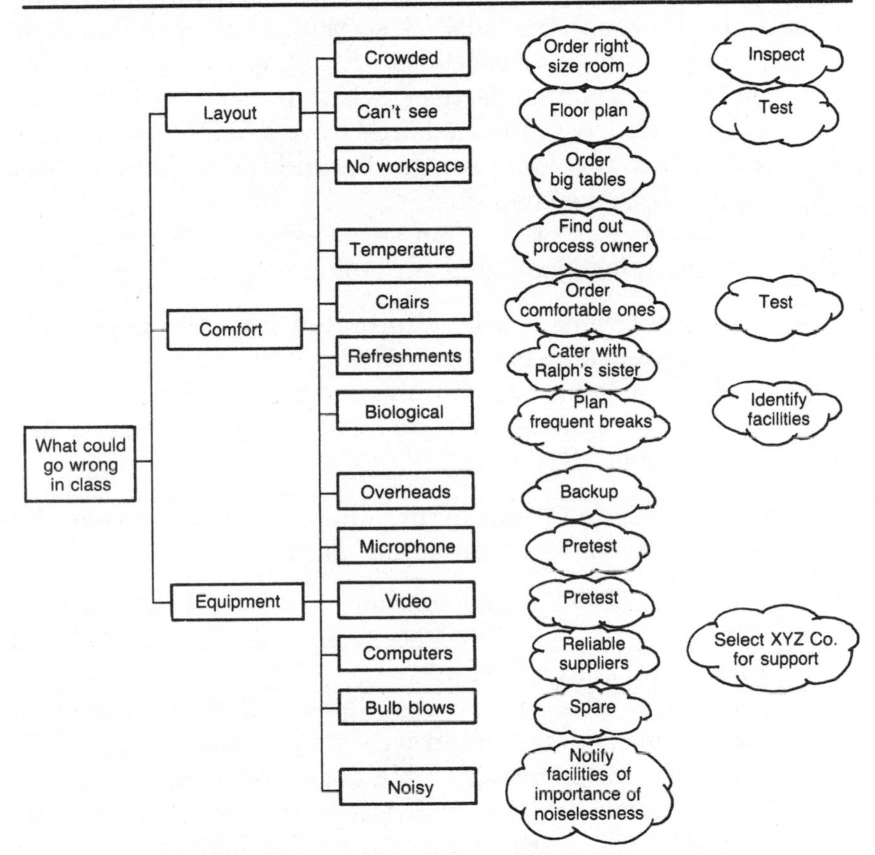

Workshop on the PDPC

A team doing a PDPC will need the following supplies.

1. Roll of butcher paper.
2. One scissor.
3. Pens (one per participant).
4. One ruler.

Arrow Diagram

The arrow diagram can aid in improving a plan and reducing plan completion time. The arrow diagram focuses attention on the flow of a plan and the time required to complete a plan. The flow of a plan is improved through the flowchart section of an arrow diagram. The completion time of a plan is optimized through the network section of an arrow diagram. Both sections will be discussed in this chapter.

The arrow diagram is used when project activities are well-defined, clearly sequenced, and have a definite beginning and end. The arrow diagram can be updated as new project information becomes available.

The flowchart section of an arrow diagram helps answer the following questions about an action plan:

1. Which actions can be eliminated from the plan (non-value-added steps)?
2. Which action's completion time can be reduced?
3. Which actions can be completed in parallel, as opposed to sequentially?

The network section of an arrow diagram helps answer the following questions about an action plan:

1. What is the expected completion date for the plan?
2. What is the scheduled start and completion date for each action in the plan?
3. Which actions must be completed within the scheduled time so the overall plan will not be delayed?
4. Which actions have flexible completion times?
5. How much flexible completion time do these actions have so the overall plan will not be delayed?

Relationship between the Arrow Diagram and PERT/CPM and the Gantt Chart

PERT (program evaluation and review technique) and CPM (critical path method) facilitate understanding the effects of deviations from a plan with respect to the completion time of the entire plan. Like the arrow diagram, PERT/CPM is used when plan actions are well-defined, clearly sequenced, and have a definite beginning and end. A PERT/CPM analysis can be updated as new project information becomes available.

Unlike the arrow diagram, PERT/CPM does not focus attention on which actions can be eliminated from a plan, which actions can have a reduction in their completion times, or which actions can be processed in parallel. In other words, PERT/CPM assumes an optimal plan for a stable system. Figure 3–30 shows the actions and network of a PERT/CPM diagram. This type of network will be discussed in detail in this chapter.

A Gantt chart, a scheduling method, highlights the beginning and ending times for each section of a plan and the overlapping sections of a plan. However, a Gantt chart cannot show the effect of deviations from a plan with respect to the completion time of the entire plan. Also, a Gantt chart does not show immediate predecessor relationships as effectively as a PERT/CPM diagram. The Gantt chart is used when the actions in a plan are well-defined, clearly sequenced, and have a definite beginning and end. A Gantt chart can be updated as new project information becomes available. Unlike the ar-

FIGURE 3–30
Arrow Diagram

Actions

Action list for buying a business

Action	Description	Immediate predecessor
A	Prepare list of potential investors	———
B	Analyze financial records of business	———
C	Develop business plan	B
D	Submit business plan to potential investors	A,C

Network

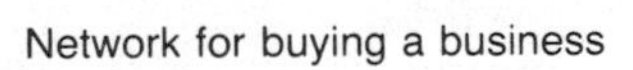
Network for buying a business

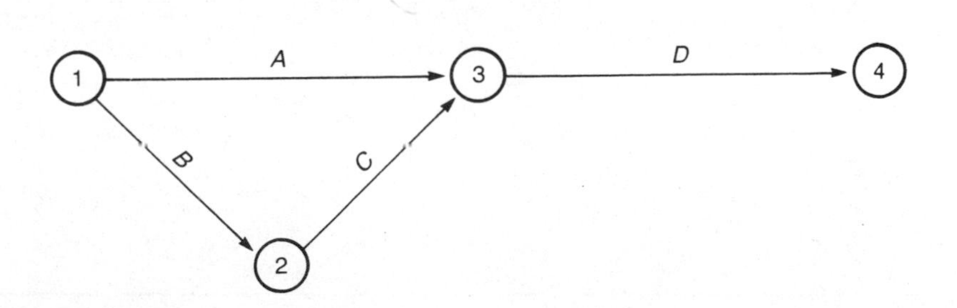

row diagram, a Gantt chart does not focus attention on which actions can be eliminated from a plan, which actions can have a reduction in their completion times, or which actions can be processed in parallel. A Gantt chart assumes an optimal plan for a stable system. Figure 3–31 shows a Gantt chart.

Some Symbols Needed to Prepare the Network Section of an Arrow Diagram

The network section of an arrow diagram requires the use of several symbols and terms. An action is denoted by an arrow. The beginning and end of an action are indicated by circles, called nodes, with node identification numbers in them. A smaller node number must be used at the beginning of an action then at the end of an action. Consequently, $i < j$ for the action defined by node i and node j. Figure 3–32 shows action A, which begins at node 1 and ends at node 2.

Two different actions cannot be defined by the same pair of nodes because they would be indistinguishable in an arrow diagram network. For example, actions A and B shown in Figure 3–33 would be confused in an arrow diagram network because they both begin with node 1 and end with node 2. Consequently, a dummy action, which is depicted by a dashed arrow, must be used so every action in an arrow diagram network is defined by a unique combination of beginning and

FIGURE 3–31
Gantt Chart for Buying a Business

		Time Frame		*(Month/19XX)*	
Activity	*Person Responsible*	*Jan.*	*Feb.*	*March*	*Comments*
(A) Develop list sources for funding	HG	x.x			
(B) Analyze financial records of business	CN	x.x			
(C) Develop business plan (e.g., sales)	CN		x.x		
(D) Submit proposal to lending institution	HG			x.x	

FIGURE 3–32
Symbols and Terms

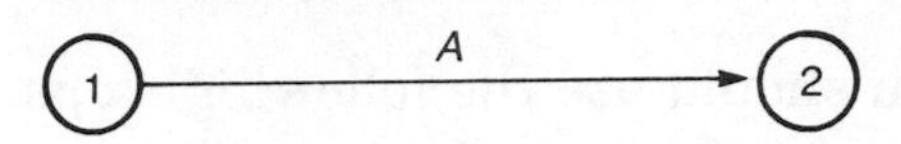

FIGURE 3–33
Wrong Activity Representation

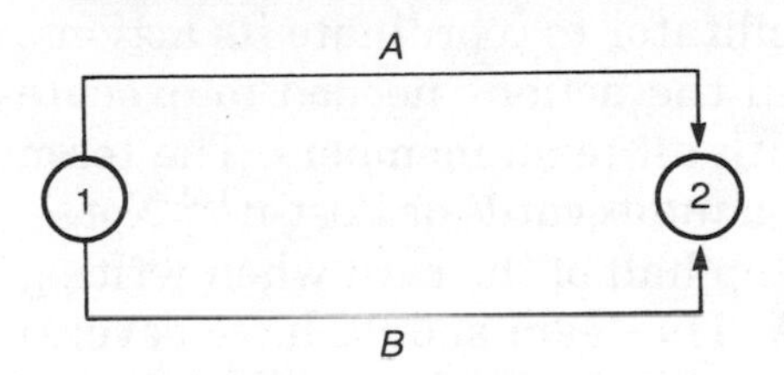

ending nodes. Figure 3–34 shows how a dummy action can be used for the network shown in Figure 3–33 so actions A and B are unique.

Construction

Arrow diagrams have two sections: a flowchart section that focuses attention on reducing the number of actions required to complete a plan and the amount of time to complete each

FIGURE 3–34
Dummy Activities

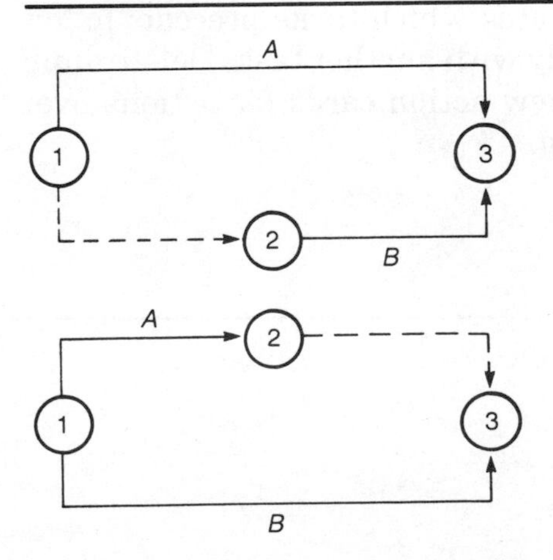

action in the plan, and a network section that focuses attention on minimizing the amount of time to complete all the actions in a plan.

A team scheduling a plan should use the following steps to construct the flowchart section of an arrow diagram.

1. Management selects the plan to be scheduled.

2. Management identifies a team appropriate to schedule the plan.

3. The team selects a facilitator to coordinate its actions.

4. The team identifies all the actions needed to execute the plan by brainstorming with all team members. The team facilitator writes the actions on index cards or Post-it™ Notes. The facilitator uses only the top half of the card when writing the action, as in Figure 3–35. The team should have several packages of cards on hand because many ideas will be generated and one card will be needed for each action.

5. The team answers the following questions.

a. Are all actions needed in the plan? Omit nonvalue-added actions.

b. Can any action have its completion time reduced? Reduce completion times.

c. Can any action be processed in parallel with any other action? Process actions in parallel.

6. The team's facilitator arranges the cards on a large surface, such as butcher paper, so the sequencing of tasks defines the positions of the cards with respect to each other. The order of the cards indicates which tasks precede, follow, or can be done simultaneously with another task. Delete duplicate action cards and add new action cards for actions overlooked during brainstorming.

FIGURE 3–35
Action Card Format

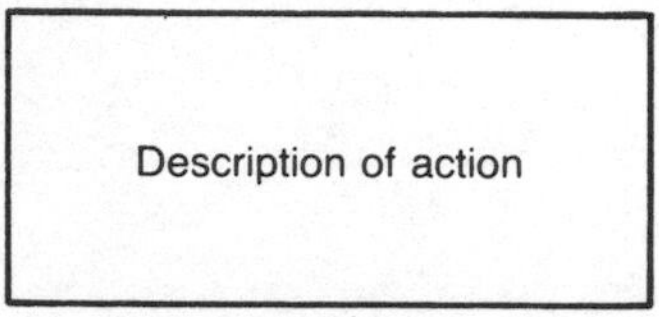

Description of action

7. The team connects the final arrangement of numbered action cards with arrows (hence the name *arrow diagram*).

Example

The following example should be helpful in understanding how to make the flowchart section of an arrow diagram.

1. Indicate the immediate predecessor(s) for each action, as in Figure 3–36.
2. Construct the arrow diagram flowchart, as shown in Figure 3–37, that represents the sequencing of actions shown in Figure 3–36.

If a team performs steps 1 through 7, it will be able to answer the following questions:

1. Which actions can be eliminated from the plan (non-value-added steps)?
2. Which action's completion time can be reduced?
3. Which actions can be completed in parallel, as opposed to serially?

The flowchart section of the arrow diagram focuses on improving the plan.

FIGURE 3–36
Immediate Predecessor for Actions

Actions A and B can begin at any time.
Action B must precede action C.
Actions A and C must precede action D.

Action List for Buying a Business

Action	*Description*	*Immediate Predecessor*
A	Prepare list of potential investors	—
B	Analyze financial records of business	—
C	Develop business plan	B
D	Submit business plan to potential investors	A,C

FIGURE 3–37
Arrow Diagram Flowchart

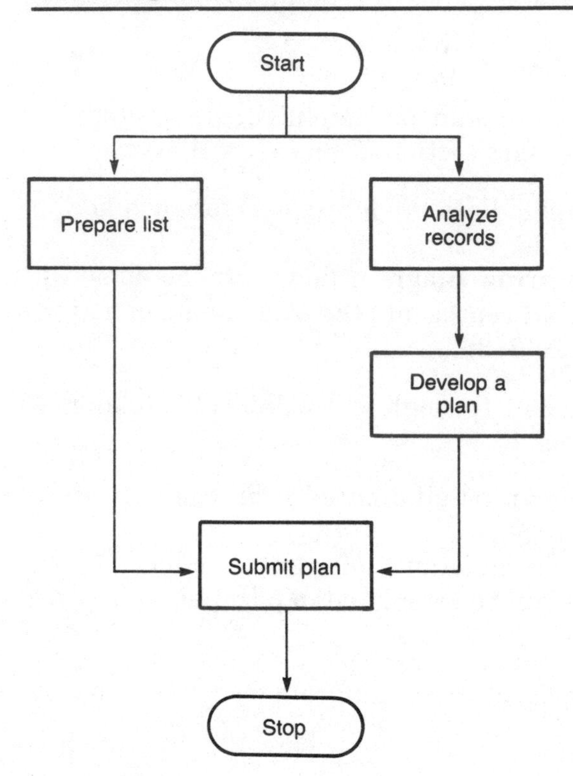

A team developing the time schedule for a plan should use the following steps to construct the network section of an arrow diagram:

1. Construct the arrow diagram network. Use dummy actions where necessary when constructing the arrow diagram network. Figure 3–38 shows a list of actions with immediate predecessors. Figure 3–39 shows the arrow diagram network needed to portray the actions shown in Figure 3–38. A list of actions[3] with immediate predecessors is shown in Figure 3–40. Figure 3–41 shows the arrow diagram network for the actions shown in Figure 3–40.

2. Estimate the average amount of time to complete each action and record the estimate on the bottom side of each

FIGURE 3–38
Action List and Immediate Predecessors

Action	*Immediate Predecessor*
A	—
B	A
C	B
D	C
E	C
F	C
G	D,E,F

action's arrow. A team can estimate the average amount of time to complete an action by using the following formula:

$$t = \frac{a + 4m + b}{6}, \text{ where}$$

t = the estimated average amount of time to complete an action
a = the time to complete an action if all goes exactly as planned (optimistic time)
m = the time to complete an action under normal conditions (most probable time)
b = the time to complete an action if significant problems occur (pessimistic time).

Note: *a, m,* and *b* are "guesstimated" by an expert about the action to be completed.

FIGURE 3–39
Arrow Diagram Network Requiring Dummy Actions

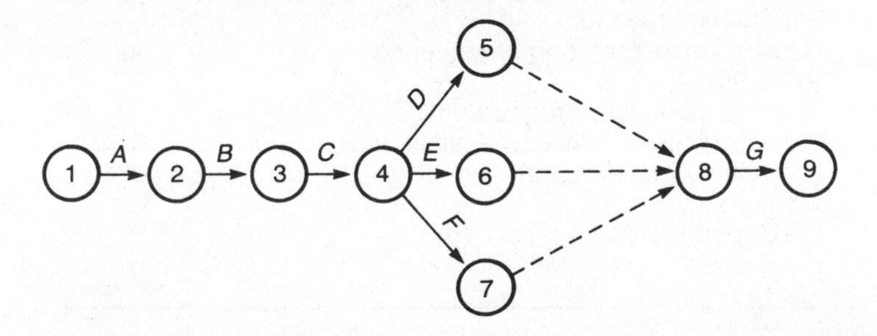

Action time estimates should *not* be: (1) related to preceding and following actions, and (2) overestimated for safety's sake. Action time estimates should: (1) consider weekends and holidays (some actions can continue while the organization is shut down, for example, aging and burn-in), and (2) consider the weather and other natural phenomena (for example, some actions cannot be performed in rain). Figure 3–42 shows the arrow diagram network with times for the actions shown in Figure 3–40.

3. Determine the critical path through the network. A *path* is a sequence of connected actions that goes from the starting node to the ending node. A *critical path* is a sequence of connecting actions that goes from the starting node to the ending node and has the longest completion time of any path through the network. A *critical action* is any action on the critical path. Delays in any action on the critical path will delay the entire project. If the total time to complete a plan is to be decreased, then the time to complete one or more critical actions must be decreased.

The calculations required to determine the critical path are as follows:

1. Earliest start time (EST): earliest time an action can be started given its predecessors.

FIGURE 3–40
Plan Action List

Action	*Description*	*Immediate Predecessors*
A	R&D product design	—
B	Plan market research	—
C	Routing (manufacturing engineering)	A
D	Build prototype model	A
E	Prepare marketing brochure	A
F	Cost estimates (industrial engineering)	C
G	Preliminary product testing	D
H	Market survey	B,E
I	Pricing and forecast report	H
J	Final report	F,G,I

FIGURE 3–41
Arrow Diagram Network

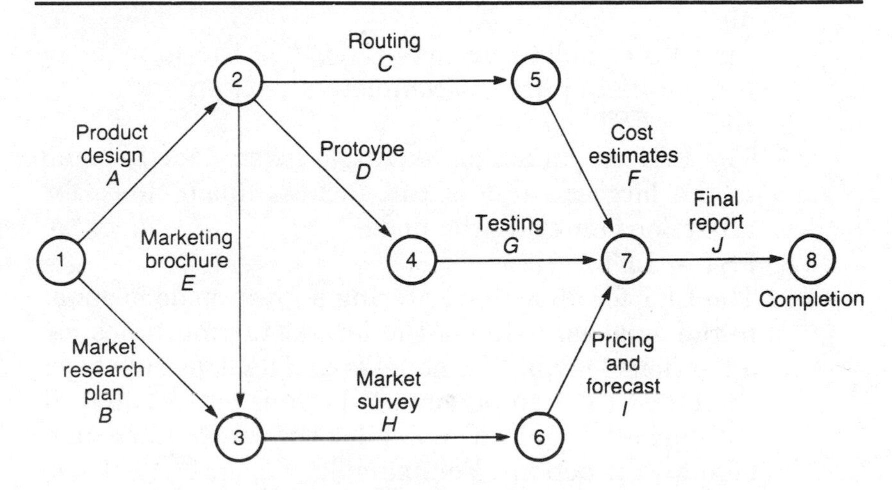

2. Latest start time (LST): latest time an action can be started if the project is to be completed on schedule.
3. Earliest finish time (EFT): earliest time an action can be completed.

FIGURE 3–42
Arrow Diagram Network with Action Times

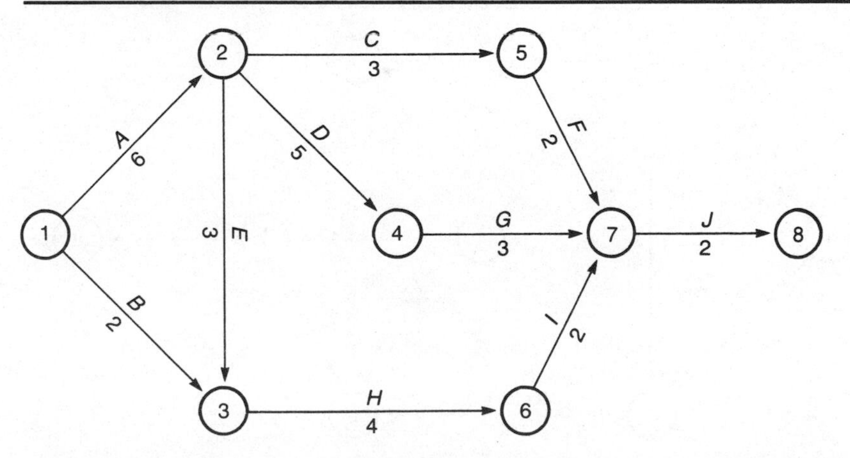

From Figure 3–41 we can see that the total time to perform all actions is 32 time units. Because several actions can be performed simultaneously, the total time to perform all actions can be shorter than 32 time periods.

4. Latest finish time (LFT): latest time an action can be finished if the project is to be completed on schedule.
5. Time to complete an action (t): t is the number of time units required to complete an action.
6. EFT = EST + t.
7. The EST for an action leaving a given node is equal to the largest value of the earliest finish times for all actions entering the node.
8. LST = LFT − t.
9. The LFT for an action entering a given node is equal to the smallest value of the latest starting times for all actions leaving the node. Logically, this rule says the latest time an action can be finished is equal to the earliest (smallest) value for the latest start time of following actions. For example, Figure 3–43 shows the arrow diagram from Figure 3–42 with ESTs and EFTs. Figure 3–44 shows the arrow diagram from Figure 3–42 with LSTs and LFTs.

FIGURE 3–43
Arrow Diagram with ESTs and EFTs

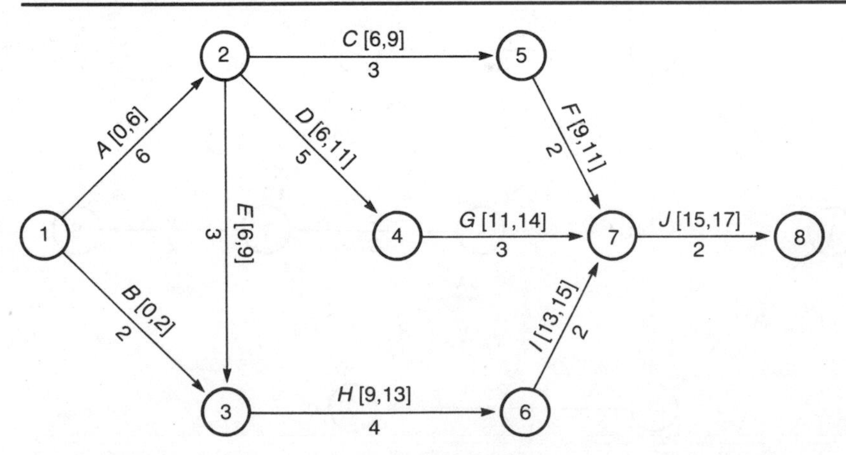

The first number in each set of brackets is the EST and the second number is the EFT.

FIGURE 3–44
Arrow Diagram with LSTs and LFTs

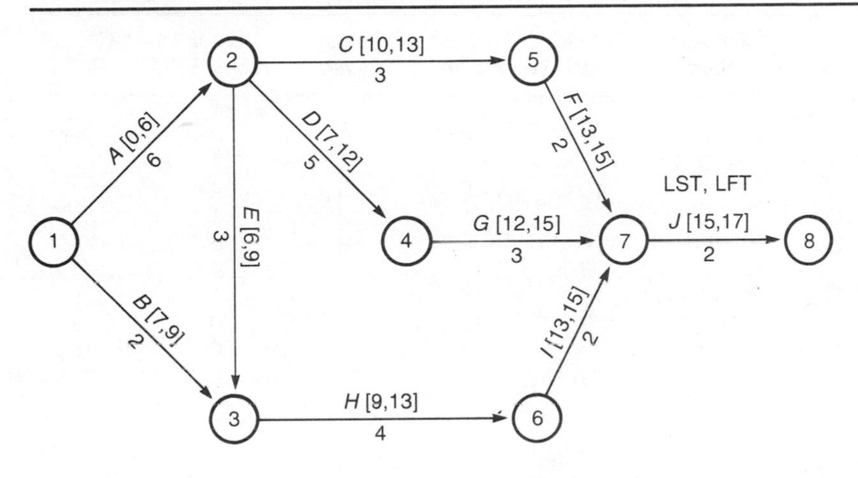

10. Slack: the amount of time an action can be delayed without delaying the entire project. If an action is on the critical path, then it has no slack time; slack = 0.
11. Slack = LST − EST = LFT − EFT. For example, the actions with slack time in Figure 3–42 are shown in Figure 3–45. The critical path is comprised of the path whose actions have no slack time, as shown in Figure 3–45.

4. Schedule the final plan.

The above steps will help a team answer the following questions about a plan:

1. What is the expected project completion date?
2. What is the scheduled start and completion date for each action?
3. Which actions must be completed in the scheduled time so the overall project will not be delayed?
4. Which actions have flexible completion times?
5. How much flexible completion time do the actions have so the overall project will not be delayed?

FIGURE 3–45
Actions with Slack Time

Action	*Earliest Start*	*Latest Start*	*Earliest Finish*	*Latest Finish*	*Slack (LS − ES)*	*Critical Path?*
A	0	0	6	6	0	Yes
B	0	7	2	9	7	
C	6	10	9	13	4	
D	6	7	11	12	1	
E	6	6	9	9	0	Yes
F	9	13	11	15	4	
G	11	12	14	15	1	
H	9	9	13	13	0	Yes
I	13	13	15	15	0	Yes
J	15	15	17	17	0	Yes

The first number in each set of brackets is the EST and the second number is the EFT.

THe critical path is A,E,H,I,J.

The latest finish time for the project is 17 time periods; LFT = 17.

The network section of an arrow diagram focuses on minimizing the time needed to complete a plan. An integrated flowchart of how to construct an arrow diagram is shown in Figure 3–46. Figure 3–47 illustrates both sections of an arrow diagram.

Workshop on the Arrow Diagram

A team working on an arrow diagram will need the following supplies:

1. One roll of butcher paper.
2. Several packages of 3 × 5 cards or Post-it™ Notes.
3. One scissor.
4. Pens (one per participant).
5. One ruler.
6. One calculator.

Summary

As we have shown, the PDPC and the arrow diagram result in a time-sequenced action plan that considers contingencies for required actions. To assure the greatest possibility of suc-

FIGURE 3–46
Integrated Flowchart of How to Construct an Arrow Diagram

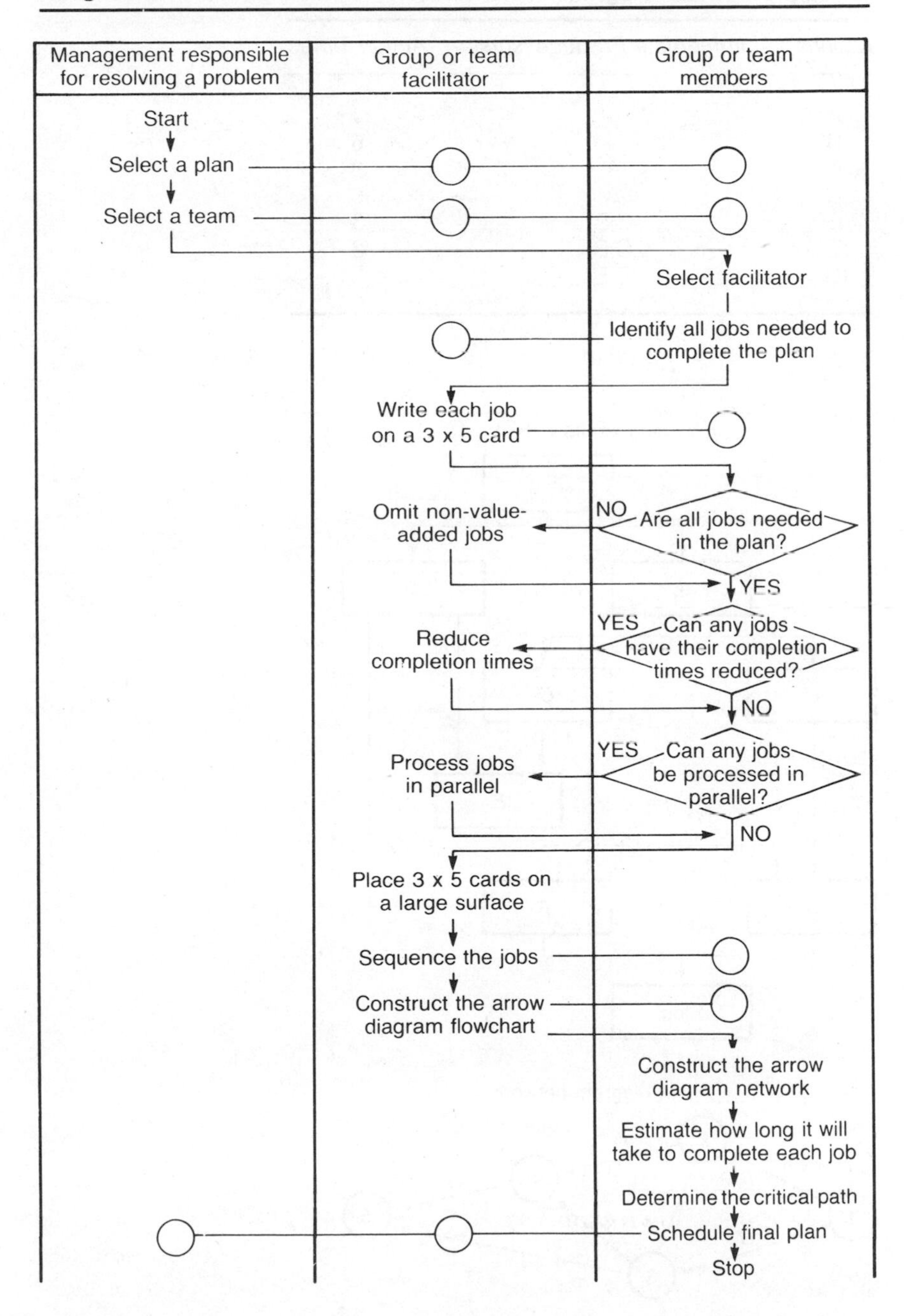

FIGURE 3–47
A Complete Arrow Diagram

Actions	*Immediate Predecessors*	*Action Times*
A	—	4
B	—	6
C	A	2
D	A	6
E	C,B	3
F	C,B	3
G	D,E	5

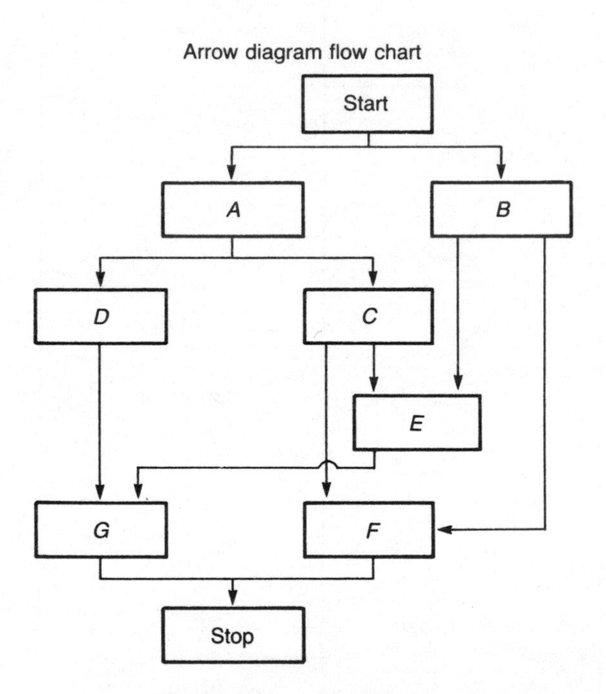

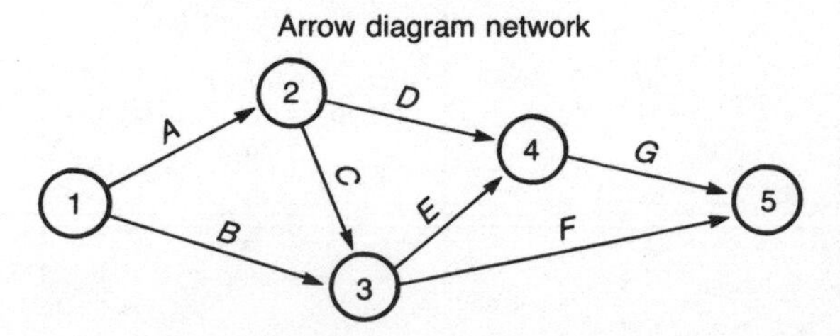

FIGURE 3–47 (*concluded*)

1. The critical path is A-D-G.

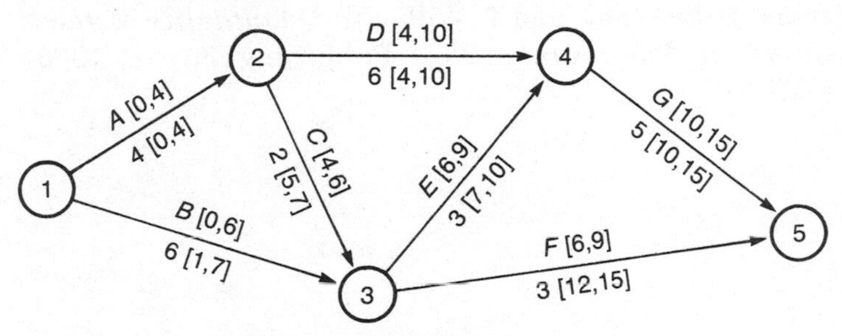

2. The critical path actions require 15 months.
3. The plan is optimal for a stable system.

cess, all action plans should consider issues such as methods, tools, training, people, processes, and time.

CHAPTER SUMMARY

This chapter presents detailed instructions for constructing a plan to be used in the PDSA cycle to decrease the difference between customer needs and process performance. The chapter explains the three phases of planning: (1) identify product or process problems whose resolution will decrease the difference between customer's needs and process performance, (2) determine the actions and resources needed to resolve the product or process problem discovered in phase one, and (3) develop contingency plans and timing for the actions stated in phase two. The seven management tools form a powerful system for planning quality improvement efforts in any area of business.

ENDNOTES

1. Post-it™ Notes is a registered trademark of the 3M Corporation.
2. PDPC is a close relative of failure mode and failure effects analysis (FMFEA). The only significant difference between PDPC and

FMFEA is that a PDPC chart is appended onto the right-most portion of a systematic diagram, whereas a FMFEA chart stands alone.

3. S. Anderson, D. Sweeney, and T. Williams, *Quantitative Methods for Business* (St. Paul, Minn.: West Publishing, 3d ed., 1985), pp. 546–53.

CHAPTER 4

EDUCATIONAL PROGRAM FOR PLANNING WITH THE SEVEN MANAGEMENT TOOLS

STRUCTURE

Education in the seven management tools should include formal in-class lectures and practice sessions in which participants divide into teams to develop a plan for solving a problem. Each practice team should form a task force and select an actual problem to solve using the seven management tools. Task force members should prepare interim and final reports. The last day of class should be devoted to a symposium in which each task force presents its plan for solving the problem. The managers of all task force team members should be invited to the symposium.

Session Timetables

The first class session of a seminar on "Planning with the Seven Management Tools" should contain: an overview of the seminar (including purpose and objectives), the selection of task force problems, and a lecture and practice session on the affinity diagram. A typical timetable for the first session can be seen in Figure 4–1. A typical timetable for subsequent sessions can be seen in Figure 4–2. At the final class session, each task force presents its plan for solving its problem.

FIGURE 4–1
Timetable for First Class Session

Time	*Topic*
9:00–10:30	Overview of planning using the seven management tools
10:30–11:00	Break
11:00–12:00	Overview of planning using the seven management tools
12:00–1:00	Lunch
1:00–2:00	Selection of task force problem
2:00–2:30	Lecture on affinity diagram
2:30–3:00	Break
3:00–4:00	Practice problem on the affinity diagram
4:00–4:30	Team presentations on: What we learned about the affinity diagram? What we learned about our problem?
4:30–5:00	Questions and answers

FIGURE 4–2
Timetable for Subsequent Class Sessions on Each of the Seven Management Tools

Time	*Topic*
9:00–10:30	Lecture on today's tool
10:30–11:00	Break
11:00–12:00	Practice problem on today's tool
12:00–1:00	Lunch
1:00–2:00	Team presentations on: What we learned about today's tool? What we learned about our problem?
2:00–3:00	Task force presentations of tools discussed in the prior class
3:00–3:30	Break
3:30–4:30	Continue task force presentations
4:30–5:00	General discussion, and questions and answers

Practice Problem Activity Sheets

Team activity sheets for practice problem selection and each of the seven management tools are shown in Figures 4–3 through 4–10.

FIGURE 4–3
Selection of Practice Problem

Purpose of workshop: The purpose of this workshop is for team members to select a practice problem through which they can learn and practice how to use the seven management tools.

Time for team to reconvene with class: ______________________

Team facilitator: ______________________

Team recorder: ______________________

Team spokesperson: ______________________

Process of practice problem selection:

- Complex and long-standing cross-departmental problem.
- No easily recognizable solution to problem.
- Varied opinions on problem.
- No logical organization of ideas relating to problem.
- No quick fix to solve problem.
- Management will commit time and resources to develop long-term solution to problem.

Hints for practice problem selection:

- All team members should contribute their perspective on the problem.
- Problem should not be so large in scope that the team cannot make progress in solving it; for example, world hunger, solid waste disposal.
- Problem should be complex enough so that all seven management tools are needed for solution.
- Problem has no right or wrong solution.
- Team members should have the authority to act on the plan to solve the problem.

Process to select the problem:

- Brainstorm a list of possible problems.
- Clarify each problem on the list for common understanding among team members.
- Screen each problem against the criteria stated in the "Hints" section above.
- Write the problem on a flip chart and post it on the wall.

Possible problems to consider:

- Barriers to losing weight.
- Barriers to accurate sales forecasting.
- Barriers to efficient mail distribution.
- Barriers to driving out fear in the workplace.
- What must be done to have constructive performance improvement in the workplace?
- What must be done to move toward a sole source of supply for any given item?

FIGURE 4–4
Affinity Diagram Workshop

Purpose of workshop: The purpose of this workshop is for team members to practice using the affinity diagram on the problem they selected to work on.

Time for team to reconvene with class: ______________________

Team facilitator: ______________________

Team recorder: ______________________

Team spokesperson: ______________________

Process of using the affinity diagram:

- Select a team facilitator, recorder, and spokesperson. These three jobs can be filled by the same or different people.
- Choose a method for data collection; that is, brainstorming or open discussion.
- Follow the steps on the integrated flowchart in Figure 3–3.
- The team's spokesperson should be prepared to discuss:
  1. What the team learned about the problem.
  2. What the team learned about the affinity diagram.

Hints for constructing the affinity diagram:

- Use a marker when writing on the cards or Post-it™ Notes; print darkly so the words can be read from a distance.
- Do not talk when clustering the cards or notes.

The problem our team selected to work on is: ______________________

____

____

______________________.

Cluster heading list:

1. ______________________
2. ______________________
3. ______________________
4. ______________________
5. ______________________
6. ______________________
7. ______________________
8. ______________________
9. ______________________
10. ______________________

Team members:

1.	4.
2.	5.
3.	6

FIGURE 4–5
Interrelationship Diagraph Workshop

Purpose of workshop: The purpose of this workshop is for team members to practice using the interrelationship diagraph on the problem they selected to work on.

Time for team to reconvene with class: ____________________

Team facilitator: ____________________

Team recorder: ____________________

Team spokesperson: ____________________

Process of using the interrelationship diagraph:

- Select a team facilitator, recorder, and spokesperson. These three jobs can be filled by the same or different people.
- If your team is going to prepare an interrelationship diagraph from the header cards from the affinity diagram workshop, prepare Post-it™ Notes for each cluster heading and the problem statement.
- Follow the steps on the integrated flowchart in Figure 3–5.
- The team's spokesperson should be prepared to discuss:
  1. What the team learned about the problem.
  2. What the team learned about the interrelationship diagraph.

Hints for constructing the interrelationship diagraph:

- Use a pencil when writing the arrows so they can be changed or erased.
- Tape blank flip chart paper on wall as a work surface.
- Arrows can go in only one direction.
- Don't write on the wall.

FIGURE 4–6
Systematic Diagram Workshop

Purpose of workshop: The purpose of this workshop is for team members to practice using the systematic diagram on the problem they selected.

Time for team to reconvene with class: ____________________

Team facilitator: ____________________

Team recorder: ____________________

Team spokesperson: ____________________

Process of using the systematic diagram:

- Select a team facilitator, recorder, and spokesperson. These three jobs can be filled by the same or different people.
- Follow the steps on the integrated flowchart in Figure 3–9.
- The team's spokesperson should be prepared to discuss:
  1. What the team learned about the problem.
  2. What the team learned about the systematic diagram.

Hints for constructing the systematic diagram:

- Wait before drawing the lines onto the systematic diagram; team members may want to reposition the actions.
- Use a large work space.
- The last (most actionable) items in each row should line up in the same column.
- Write all action items in the positive sense.

Figure 4–7
Matrix Diagram Workshop

Purpose of workshop: The purpose of this workshop is for team members to practice using the matrix diagram on the problem they selected.

Time for team to reconvene with class: ______________________

Team facilitator: ______________________

Team recorder: ______________________

Team spokesperson: ______________________

Process of using the matrix diagram:

- Select a team facilitator, recorder, and spokesperson. These three jobs can be filled by the same or different people.
- Use an L-matrix. The rows of the L-matrix should be the action items from your team's systematic diagram and the columns of the L-matrix should be the people or resources needed to accomplish the action items.
- Use the following symbols:
  (⊙) Primary responsibility.
  (○) Secondary responsibility.
  (△) Keep informed.
- Follow the steps on the integrated flowchart in Figure 3–16.
- The team's spokesperson should be prepared to discuss:
  1. What the team learned about the problem.
  2. What the team learned about the matrix diagram.

Hint for constructing the matrix diagram:

- Tape flip chart paper or butcher paper next to the right-hand side of your team's systematic diagram to draw the L-matrix.

FIGURE 4–8
Glyph Workshop

Purpose of workshop: The purpose of this workshop is for team members to practice using the glyph on the problem they selected.

Time for team to reconvene with class: ______________________

Team facilitator: ______________________

Team recorder: ______________________

Team spokesperson: ______________________

Process of using the glyph:

- Select a team facilitator, recorder, and spokesperson. These three jobs can be filled by the same or different people.
- Develop data collection instrument and procedure.
- Follow the steps on the integrated flowchart in Figure 3–27.
- The team's spokesperson should be prepared to discuss:
  1. What the team learned about the problem.
  2. What the team learned about the glyph.

Hint for constructing the glyph:

- Don't allow only one team member to prepare the glyph.

FIGURE 4–9
Program Decision Process Chart Workshop

Purpose of workshop: The purpose of this workshop is for team members to practice using the PDPC on the problem they selected.

Time for team to reconvene with class: ____________________

Team facilitator: ____________________

Team recorder: ____________________

Team spokesperson: ____________________

Process of using the PDPC:

- Select a team facilitator, recorder, and spokesperson. These three jobs can be filled by the same or different people.
- Select one branch from the team's systematic diagram.
- Follow the steps on the integrated flowchart in Figure 3–28.
- The team's spokesperson should be prepared to discuss:
  1. What the team learned about the problem.
  2. What the team learned about the PDPC.

Hints for constructing the PDPC:

- Work on one action at a time.
- Develop contingency plans that are feasible to implement.

FIGURE 4–10
Arrow Diagram Workshop

Purpose of workshop: The purpose of this workshop is for team members to practice using the arrow diagram on the problem they selected.

Time for team to reconvene with class: ____________________

Team facilitator: ____________________

Team recorder: ____________________

Team spokesperson: ____________________

Process of using the arrow diagram:

- Select a team facilitator, recorder, and spokesperson. These three jobs can be filled by the same or different people.
- Follow the steps on the integrated flowchart in Figure 3–46.
- The team's spokesperson should be prepared to discuss:
  1. What the team learned about the problem.
  2. What the team learned about the arrow diagram.

Hint for constructing the arrow diagram:

- Don't allow only one team member to prepare the arrow diagram.

PROMOTION

In-house promotion of a seminar on "Planning with the Seven Management Tools" requires that information about prerequisites, target audience, seminar objectives, and methods be widely distributed through the organization's quality steering committee. The following paragraphs are examples of information that should be publicized about the seminar.

Prerequisites

The material covered in the seminar will be most appreciated by a participant who has studied, and attended seminars on, (1) understanding the Deming philosophy, as described in Figure 4–11; (2) tools and methods of the Deming philosophy (basic statistical skills), as described in Figure 4–12; and (3) team building techniques of the Deming philosophy (conflict resolution and consensus decision-making skills), as described in Figure 4–13.

Target Audience

The target audience includes all levels of management involved in planning for the improvement of quality; this should include all managers. Isolated use of the seven management tools will be ineffective; consequently, the first group of employees to receive education on the seven management tools should be top management.

Objectives

This seminar provides a participant with practical skills for planning with the seven management tools in the PDSA cycle. These planning tools can be used for developing quality improvement plans or new product designs, to name a few applications. The proper application of these planning tools, when used in the environmental setting created by the Deming philosophy, results in better planning, in less time, with increased quality. Managers attending will become familiar with the

FIGURE 4–11
Understanding the Deming Philosophy

Scope: This three-day seminar is intended for all levels of management. It presents the management philosophy of Dr. W. Edwards Deming, often called the father of modern management. The concepts presented in this seminar have been adopted by many corporations, both nationally and internationally, and are widely held responsible for the remarkable success of many organizations.

Objectives: Participants in this seminar will come to understand the organization as a collection of interrelated processes, each being a customer and vendor to other processes. They will be introduced to the major elements of the Deming philosophy, including Dr. Deming's Fourteen Points for management. Participants will be shown how Dr. Deming's Fourteen Points for management are driven by the quest for continuous and never-ending improvement of all processes connected with an organization and how they cause the following chain reaction: improved processes, less rework, higher quality, higher productivity, lower unit cost, greater price flexibility, increased market share, increased profit, and more secure jobs for all employees.

Methodology: Groups of participants will meet for 12 90-minute sessions over a three-day period. Discussions will utilize overhead transparencies, group demonstrations, videotapes, handouts, and workshops. Each participant will be provided with a copy of *The Deming Guide to Quality and Competitive Position,* by Howard Gitlow and Shelly Gitlow, and a complete set of the overhead transparencies used during the discussions so tedious note taking may be avoided and a permanent reference may be retained.

Seminar Outline:

Part 1—Introduction

- The plight of American industry today
- The chain reaction between process improvement and quality, productivity, and competitive position
- Who is W. Edwards Deming?
- Concept of a process
- The extended process
- Quality of design, conformance, and performance
- Types of variation in a process
- The bead box experiment
- The funnel experiment
- Responsibility for process variation
- A System of Profound Knowledge

Part 2—The Fourteen Points

1. Create constancy of purpose toward improvement of product and service, with the aim to become competitive and to stay in business and to provide jobs.
2. Adopt the new philosophy. We are in a new economic age. Western management must awaken to the challenge, must learn its responsibilities, and take on leadership for change.
3. Cease dependence on inspection to achieve quality. Eliminate the need for inspection on a mass basis by building quality into the product in the first place.

FIGURE 4–11 *(concluded)*

4. End the practice of awarding business on the basis of price tag. Instead, minimize total cost. Move toward a single supplier for any one item, on a long-term relationship of loyalty and trust.
5. Improve constantly and forever the system of production and service, to improve quality and productivity, and thus constantly decrease costs.
6. Institute training on the job.
7. Institute leadership (see point 12). The aim of leadership should be to help people and machines and gadgets to do a better job. Leadership of management needs an overhaul, as well as leadership of production workers.
8. Drive out fear, so everyone may work effectively for the company.
9. Break down barriers between departments. People in research, design, sales, and production must work as a team to foresee production and use problems that may be encountered with the product or service.
10. Eliminate slogans, exhortations, and targets for the work force asking for zero defects and new levels of productivity.

11a. Eliminate work standards (quotas) on the factory floor. Substitute leadership.

11b. Eliminate management by objectives. Eliminate management by numbers, numerical goals. Substitute leadership.

12a. Remove barriers that rob the hourly worker of his or her right to pride of workmanship. The responsibility of supervisors must be changed from sheer numbers to quality.

12b. Remove barriers that rob people in management and in engineering of their right to pride of workmanship. This means abolishment of the annual or merit rating and of management by objective, management by the numbers.

13. Institute a vigorous program of education and self-improvement.
14. Put everybody in the company to work to accomplish the transformation. The transformation is everybody's job.

Part 3—Labor/management relations—changing the corporate culture
Part 4—Relating each of the Fourteen Points to the reduction of variation
Part 5—How to begin
- Initial training for management
- Steering committee formation
- Having the steering committee members answer the questions in Chapter 5 of *Out of the Crisis*
- Functions of the steering committee

FIGURE 4–12
Tools and Methods of the Deming Philosophy

Scope: This three-day seminar is designed to follow "Understanding the Deming Philosophy." It is intended for all levels of management, plus suppliers. It presents the powerful tools and techniques of the Deming philosophy. These methods have been adopted and are widely used by many organizations, both domestically and internationally. The proper application of these tools, when used in the environmental setting created by the Deming philosophy,

FIGURE 4–12 *(concluded)*

results in increased quality, increased productivity, decreased unit costs, increased price flexibility, increased market share, increased profit, and more secure jobs for all employees.

Objectives: Participants will learn basic statistical quality control techniques as they relate to the Deming philosophy. They will be exposed to applications in manufacturing, service, administration, and sales. Managers attending will become familiar with the tools and techniques required to pursue Dr. Deming's Fourteen Points.

Methodology: Groups of participants will meet for 12 90-minute sessions over a three-day period. Discussions will utilize overhead transparencies, group demonstrations, videotapes, handouts, and workshops. Each participant will be provided with a complete set of the overhead transparencies used during the discussions so tedious note taking may be avoided and a permanent reference may be retained.

Seminar Outline:

Part 1—Background
- Review of the extended process and quality
- Review of the Deming philosophy

Part 2—Basic concepts
- Defining and documenting a process
- Basic statistics
  - Types of data
  - Frequency distributions
  - Histograms and bar charts
  - Run charts
  - Mean and median
  - Range and standard deviation
  - Proportion

Part 3—Control charts
- Attribute control charts
  - p-charts
  - c-charts
  - u-charts
- Variables control charts
  - xbar and R charts
  - Individuals and moving range charts
  - Other control charts

Part 4—Stabilizing and improving a process
- Brainstorming
- Cause-and-effect diagrams
- Check sheets
- Pareto diagrams
- Stratification
- Other tools

Part 5—Process capability and specifications

Part 6—Inspection policy and acceptance sampling (time permitting)

FIGURE 4–13
Team-Building Techniques of the Deming Philosophy

Scope: This two-day seminar is intended for all levels of management. It presents the tools and techniques for team building. These tools and methods include conflict resolution and consensus decision-making.

Objectives: Participants will develop their team skills. They will be introduced to conflict resolution and consensus decision-making, in the context to Dr. Deming's Fourteen Points for management. Participants will be shown how Dr. Deming's Fourteen Points for management require cooperation and a team/family view of the organization.

Methodology: Groups of participants will meet for eight 90-minute sessions over a two-day period. Discussions will utilize overhead transparencies, group demonstrations, videotapes, handouts, and workshops. Each participant will be provided with a complete set of the overhead transparencies used during the discussions so tedious note taking may be avoided and a permanent reference may be retained.

Seminar Outline:

Part 1—Introduction to team building
Part 2—Improving individual conflict resolution skills and managing group conflict
Part 3—Improving individual communication skills and managing group communication
Part 4—Developing consensus in groups
Part 5—Improving group problem-solving skills
Part 6—Improving meeting management skills
Part 7—Team building

seven management tools required to develop quality improvement plans that are important in pursuing Dr. Deming's Fourteen Points.

Method

Classroom-style lectures on each of the seven management tools will be presented to participants. After each classroom presentation, the participants will break into small groups to practice the tool just discussed, thereby facilitating learning of the tool.

Brochure

A sample promotional brochure for a seminar on planning with the seven management tools is shown in Figure 4–14.

This brochure may be copied without the permission of the publisher.

INSTRUCTIONS TO THE SEMINAR LEADER

A seminar on planning with the seven management tools requires the following supplies, audiovisual equipment, and room configuration.

Supplies

- Five packages of 3 × 5 cards or Post-it™ Notes per team.
- One flip chart per team plus one for the seminar leader.
- One roll of butcher paper.
- One scissor per team.
- One pencil per participant.

FIGURE 4–14
Sample Brochure

Planning with the Seven Management Tools

A seminar designed to develop critical planning skills for managers

FIGURE 4–14 *(continued)*

Planning with the Seven Management Tools

Benefits

This seminar is a must for any organization that is ready to go beyond the **basic QC** tools and learn to use the next set of tools—the **Seven Management** tools. The tools are presented in a project planning context. Hence, the seminar is also for anyone who has to plan and coordinate projects of any type. Over half of the course is hands-on workshops in which participants use the seven tools. The goal of "Planning with the Seven Management Tools" is to provide team leaders and project managers with an effective planning model for solving problems—even the complex, unwieldly, time-consuming ones. The seven tools are especially useful for projects and issues that have not responded to traditional solutions and those which require heavy team involvement.

Upon completion participants will be able to:

- ☐ know and use each of the seven management tools.
- ☐ define the purpose, value, and application of each of the tools.
- ☐ facilitate the use of the seven tools in groups chartered with projects and/or resolving issues.
- ☐ select the appropriate tools to use based on the problem and/or its stage in the resolution cycle.
- ☐ identify and remove barriers and roadblocks that may be encountered in using the seven tools.
- ☐ effectively plan a project.
- ☐ use these tools in other aspects of one's work.

Who Should Attend

Managers, project leaders, and quality team leaders responsible for planning and completing specific projects and/or the resolution of complex issues. This seminar is especially powerful when members of a management team or task team can attend together. These teams can get an organized start using the tools as a group and a start on working their project.

Topics Addressed

DAY 1

- ☐ The Seven Management Tools:
  - their origin
  - how these tools are used in a Deming framework
  - their relationship to quality
- ☐ Consensus decision making
- ☐ A model for planning:
  - how each tool fits
  - an overview of the seven management tools
- ☐ Affinity Diagram*
- ☐ The Interrelationship Diagraph*
- ☐ Summary

DAY 2

- ☐ Systematic Diagram*
- ☐ Matrix Diagram*
- ☐ Perceptual Mapping* and Glyph*
- ☐ Process Decision Program Chart (PDPC) analysis*
- ☐ Arrow Diagram*
- ☐ Other applications and uses for the seven management tools

***To increase learning and understanding, these topics are covered as a workshop/small group activity.**

- One pad per participant.
- Two markers per team (red and black).
- One roll of masking tape per team.
- One box of blank transparencies.

FIGURE 4–14 *(concluded)*

Registration

Attendance in this seminar is limited, so we recommend you register immediately. You will receive a written confirmation with additional information upon receipt of your registration.

Fee

The "Planning with the Seven Management Tools" seminar fee is $ _____. This fee includes:

- ☐ presentation by an expert instructor
- ☐ a course manual
- ☐ lunch each day
- ☐ morning and afternoon refreshments

Schedule

The sessions are from 8:00 a.m. to 5:00 p.m. each day. Lunch is provided and served around noon.

Seminar Location

Cancellation/Substitution Policy

On-Site Presentation

Instructor

REGISTRATION FORM

Planning with the Seven Management Tools

(Duplicate for additional registrations)

NAME ______________________

TITLE ______________________

COMPANY ______________________

ADDRESS ______________________

____

CITY __________ STATE ____ ZIP ______

PHONE (______) ______________

☐ Please register me for Planning with the Seven Management Tools

RETURN TO:

- Two grease pens for overhead transparencies per team (red and black) plus two for the seminar leader.
- One ruler per team.

Audiovisual Equipment

- Overhead projector plus extra bulb.
- Large screen.
- Wall space for teams to hang practice assignments (to be taken down after each class).

Room Configuration

The room should be broken into two sections. Section one is to be set up classroom style. Section two is to be set up so there is one table for each team. A team will contain four or five people. The tables should be as widely dispersed as possible so the teams do not disturb each other.

PUTTING IT ALL TOGETHER

Process improvement efforts focus on resolving sources of special variation, eliminating sources of system variation, and centering a process on the desired nominal level. Using the seven management tools can result in action plans that decrease the difference between customer needs and process performance by reducing process variation and centering a process on nominal.

REFERENCES

Anderson, S.; Sweeney, D.; and Williams, T. *Quantitative Methods for Business*. 3rd ed. St. Paul, Minn.: West Publishing Co., 1985.

Brassard, M. *Seven Tools for Managing and Planning*. Lawrence, Mass.: Growth Opportunity Alliance of Greater Lawrence/Quality Productivity Competitiveness, 1988.

Deming, W. E. *Out of the Crisis*. Cambridge, Mass.: Massachusetts Institute of Technology, Center for Advanced Engineering Study, 1986.

Gitlow, H., and Gitlow, S. *The Deming Guide to Quality and Competitive Position*. Englewood Cliffs, N.J.: Prentice-Hall, 1987.

Gitlow, H.; Gitlow, S.; Oppenheim, A.; and Oppenheim, R. *Tools and Methods for the Improvement of Quality*. Homewood, Ill.: Richard D. Irwin, Inc., 1989.

Ishikawa, K. *What Is Total Quality Control?: The Japanese Way*. Englewood Cliffs, N.J.: Prentice-Hall, 1985.

Ishikawa, K. "Special Issue: Seven Management Tools for QC, Reports of Statistical Application Research, Union of Japanese Scientists and Engineers." *Rep. Stat. Appl. Res., JUSE* 33, no. 2 (June 1986), ISSN 0034–4842.

Juran, J. *Juran on Leadership for Quality: An Executive Handbook*. New York: The Free Press, 1989.

Juran, J., and Gryna, F. *Juran's Quality Control Handbook*. 4th ed. New York: McGraw-Hill, 1988.

Kohn, Alfie. *No Contest*. Boston: Houghton Mifflin, 1986.

Kotler, P. *Marketing Models: A Model Building Approach*. New York: Holt, Rinehart & Winston, 1971, pp. 491–97.

Mizuno, S. *Management for Quality Improvement: The Seven New QC Tools*. Cambridge, Mass.: Productivity Press, 1988.

Ouchi, W. *The M-Form Society*. Reading, Mass.: Addison-Wesley Publishing, 1984.

Process Management International, Inc. "Training Manual on the 7 Basic Tools," pp. 11–79 through 11–83.

Reydel, M. "Master's Thesis." University of Miami, Coral Gables, Fla., 1986.

Scherkenbach, W. *The Deming Route to Quality and Productivity: Road Maps and Roadblocks* Washington, D.C.: CeePress Books, 1986.

INDEX

F

G

H

I

Q

R–S

W–Z